PAGAN
ANGER MAGIC

PAGAN ANGER MAGIC

POSITIVE TRANSFORMATIONS FROM NEGATIVE ENERGIES

Tammy Sullivan

CITADEL PRESS
Kensington Publishing Corp.
www.kensingtonbooks.com

To Regina and Holly
for their unwavering support of my vision

CITADEL PRESS BOOKS are published by

Kensington Publishing Corp.
850 Third Avenue
New York, NY 10022

All Kensington titles, imprints, and distributed lines are available at special quantity discounts for bulk purchases for sales promotions, premiums, fund-raising, educational, or institutional use. Special book excerpts or customized printings can also be created to fit specific needs. For details, write or phone the office of the Kensington special sales manager: Kensington Publishing Corp., 850 Third Avenue, New York, NY 10022, attn: Special Sales Department; phone 1-800-221-2647.

CITADEL PRESS and the Citadel logo are Reg. U.S. Pat. & TM Off.

First printing: July 2005

10 9 8 7 6 5 4 3 2 1

Printed in the United States of America

Library of Congress Control Number: 2005922704

ISBN 0-8065-2671-8

CONTENTS

PREFACE

Welcome to the results of some of the hardest years of life I have ever known. I will be forever grateful for every day of those years, for while the trip may have been a wild one, the lessons I learned were profound.

I spent many years out of control when it comes to my emotions. I loved too hard and hated too deep. As a result, I became depressed often. I frequently felt regret, due to allowing my emotions to cloud my decisions, and usually ended up making bad choices.

One day I realized I had to either allow myself to continue being out of my own control, or wake up and deal with the problems. It was all up to me. I decided that I was not about to allow my emotions to literally drive me mad. According to my personal definition of mental health, maintaining control is not optional—it is a necessity.

Controlling your sanity begins with controlling your emotions. To strive for anything less than perfect control is an invitation for imbalance.

Realizing that I had a tendency to let my emotions take over from rational thought, I began to search for help. I wanted to deal with my anger in a positive manner. I went into therapy, hoping to understand and make friends with my anger. I took medicine, hoping to balance my anger better or to erase it completely. I read books that taught that I should just swallow my anger—as if it would just go away.

I felt shortchanged by the suggestion of a passive approach to such an aggressive emotion. I felt cheated when I would read things that were more judgmental about the possession of an emotion than that of a purposeful wrong to someone or something. Emotions are not something we decide to have, they simply are. I felt as if the whole world were saying anger was wrong when it was a vital function of my humanity, and on many days it was what made me feel alive. Anger was the gut reaction that told me what was right and what was wrong. I simply could not imagine that anger could not be put to good use, since it was such a big part of me. I was tired of being ashamed of my feelings.

When nothing I read or did seemed to work or have any answers, being a Witch, I finally looked for a magical solution. Lo and behold! No books were available to guide me through the process of streamlining anger into my magical practices. No one I knew even wanted to talk about it. I found plenty relating to the use of other emotions, but everyone seemed to shy away from anger, and that was the one emotion I seemed to have a surplus of. I needed to know how to put it to use. Through trial and error, and a lot of prayer, I developed a system that worked for me—on both a spiritual level and a magical one.

While I worked out the Anger Magic system, my matron goddess, Hecate, kept throwing down new things for my examination and inclusion. Indeed, the last few months while I have been writing about what I've learned have heralded that I still have much more to learn. The frustrations and distractions I experienced while writing this book have been unparalleled. Two of my family members moved hundreds of miles away and others were facing major health problems. Two people whom I knew and loved died. Many of my days were spent in tears and worry. My emotions threatened to overwhelm my judgment. Nevertheless, once my anger was roused, a solution to any problems quickly followed.

I believe it was my matron goddess Hecate's purpose to provoke my frustrations and my anger, to see all these feelings described within the pages of this book. Moreover, she was not the only goddess to make her presence known.

While I was writing the chapter on Eris and Chaos my computer shut off halfway through and I lost all the data I had to that point. I had to begin again, and when I did, I heard the loudest thunder—only to look outside and find bright, sunny skies. The phone rang about a thousand times and it was an extremely frustrating day. Eris the goddess of Discord truly made a grand entrance, one that I am not likely to forget. As if to prove herself true to her nature, she did the same things again the very next day. I put that particular chapter behind me as quickly as I could.

However, Eris also had the ability to frustrate me to the point where it became funny. I found an odd sort of relaxation with her because there was nothing I could do to prevent her antics, except finish the work. She presented the inspirational side of herself through that episode, which is a seldom-discussed quality she possesses. I felt as if she were standing beside me and hounding me with questions: "Do you want it enough? How bad do you want it? How determined are you to finish?" These inquiries definitely roused my anger and made me even more determined to finish the task. Come Hel or high water, I would allow nothing to stand in my way.

Throughout the planning period of this book, I found the topic of anger itself was enough to provoke people. In discussions with friends, I watched in astonishment as arguments about my subject occurred. The amazing thing about the arguments is that my friends were agreeing with each other without realizing it. It was as if the very word *anger* directly presented a threat, and an appropriately aggressive response.

Throughout all of the setbacks, frustrations, and delays, rest assured that I have experienced my own anger from so many different perceptions that I feel I fully understand its purpose. To steal a line from the Boy Scouts of America, Anger Magic is about being prepared. Therefore, while this book is a good introduction to the principles of Anger Magic, it is only the beginning. The work that originates here will carry on throughout your lifetime.

Because every day heralds a new development to deal with, I depend on the exercises in this book to keep me strong. I am in control of my emotions these days. I insist on maintaining that control. Working the system, I have found that I now tend to become angry only when a severe imbalance has occurred, and I know that anger must be the emotion needed or it would not exist within me at that time.

The views presented in this book may seem unique, even controversial to some, but they are nonetheless valid and true. Some may prefer to avoid the topic of anger altogether without ever searching the text of this book to find the message inside. That is understandable. Not everyone is ready to deal with such a difficult issue.

Likewise, some may not be willing to tackle with such formidable deities as those presented here. This book will bring you face to face with the crème de la crème of destroyers, havoc-wreakers, and death goddesses. However, I think you will find they certainly have their place and are not nearly as "dangerous" as is commonly thought. The theme of anger in magical practice corresponds in some ways to that of death. Both are about moving forward and beginning again.

This book is not meant to be a beginner's guide to Witchcraft. It picks up where such guides leave off—assuming, for example, that you already understand the terms used and know about basic magical tasks such as circle casting, purging, and grounding. Anger Magic is advanced magic. It is simple, but life changing.

The ethical system employed in *Exploring Anger Magic* is flexible; therefore, it is suitable for use by many different kinds of people. I personally guarantee that if you incorporate the information in this book to master the art of controlling your anger, you will notice a difference in the power of your magic, and an improvement in the quality of your life.

Without further unnecessary commentary, what do you say we turn to page 3 and get started?

Special Thanks

Thanks to my sisters: Parthena Black for sharing her social worker's perspective, Leslie for sharing so much time editing, and Regina for reading the text over and over again.

Thanks to Rain for her amazing conceptual support in the very beginning.

A very special thanks to author Willow Polsen, for helping me get this book to the right publisher.

A special thanks to Peter Hope, for sharing his knowledge of Hecate.

I would also like to thank Christopher Sauls, for the willow meditation idea.

Thank you, Dorothy Morrison, for being such an inspiration and encouraging me. Thank you, Lexi, for your warm concern and encouragement.

In addition, the most special thank you to my husband, Terry; thank you for always believing in me, and to my daughter Elizabeth; thank you for giving Mommy the time to do what she needed to do.

I. Understanding Anger Magic

I. Working with Anger

verything in our lives relates to emotion. The foods we
favor often have a comforting quality, due to the emotion
we felt when we ate them for the first time. Likewise, the
people we surround ourselves with are similarly related with our
emotions. If we were having a terrible day when we first meet
them, we are much more likely to associate them with feeling terrible and choose not to like them. Even aromas relate to emotion.
And emotions are the driving power of magic. Our lives are
meaningless without emotion. It is the emotion elicited from an
event that creates a memory. Emotions transcend time and space
as we relive old memories or look forward to new events.

The ability to control our emotions is the first step in successful
magical practice. When we combine emotion with controlled
thought, we begin the process of obtaining our desires. Emotions
are power; they are the generators for energy.

When dealing with an emotion like anger in a magical setting,
we must be precise. Anger is volatile and chaotic, so our reaction
to it must be deliberate. It is only through careful examination and
soul searching, combined with daily efforts such as meditation and
control exercises, that we can harness the unlimited power of anger.

Anger is needed in order to strike a balance in your life. You
cannot truly know happiness without understanding anger. Likewise, you cannot truly know yourself if you ignore such an important part of your existence.

Some people have asked me, "Isn't anger magic a kind of black
magic?" They automatically assume that if you are working with
anger in a magical sense, the effect must be negative. My answer
to them is no, this is not black magic at all. We are working with

the darker side of ourselves, and we will walk the line of balance between this world and the shadow world throughout this book, but we will not stray into "black" or harmful magic. Some of the information presented later may seem questionable. In the proper context and utilized in a healthy, life-affirming manner, however, it is meant to be a positive experience. This book is also not an excuse. Just because you accept, embrace, and use your anger does not mean that you should use it for negative purposes.

You may also be wondering if it is safe to work with anger in magic. Yes, it is. Anger is a primal emotion genetically encoded within each person at birth. The first thing we need to do is rid ourselves of the idea that anger is wrong or bad. Anger is natural, and, it serves a natural purpose.

At no time will this book seek to set your ethics for you. However, you will always be informed when you will be taking karmic risk. Any information presented that has a karmic attachment, which you then attempt to perform, be advised that you do so with full knowledge of the risks.

Due to the pressure of modern times, anger can reach an unhealthy level, one that may at first be considered petty and can then grow to be difficult to control. Petty anger should be transformed in order to become useful. Righteous anger, which is natural and healthy, can be used as is.

Through the methods outlined in this book, we can transform both types of anger into raw energy, which is more suitable for most types of magical work.

Following are some frequently asked questions relating to Anger Magic. It is important to dispel widely held myths about Anger Magic right off the bat. Hence, we'll deal with some of them now.

How does Anger Magic work?

Magic contains three key elements: knowledge, need, and emotion. These elements are combined in a spell or ritual to focus your will and cause change to occur.

The universe, and everything in it, even thoughts, is made of energy. Directing or manipulating that energy is magic. Hence the old saying, "Be careful what you wish for." Wishes and daydreaming are forms of magic. When you add purpose to daydreaming or wishes, you are casting a spell. Bringing emotion into play is a powerful push and will speed things along.

Remember—magic flows, like a river. It follows the path of least resistance. Sometimes what you deem an obstacle may not be one at all. Magic will flow around it.

What are the best uses for anger in magic?

The best use for anger is to transform it into raw energy that you may direct anywhere. However, anger can also be used to shield and protect, serve justice, destroy negative traits and habits, create works of art, or inspire deeper levels of understanding.

Is anger really that powerful?

Anger has the potential and the power to reach all levels of time and space, it can and does reach beyond the grave. Anger and rage have been linked to many hauntings, suggesting that the power of rage is unparalleled.

If you are dealing with a case of righteous anger, you may employ it directly without transformation, provided you do the necessary self-examinations to determine the best use. Anger can lose a bit of its original potency in the transformation process.

Can a beginning practitioner use anger in magic?

Yes, if you feel it, you may use it. However, it takes years of practice to master Anger Magic, and you must be willing to commit to it.

In what situations should I avoid using Anger Magic?

For your own protection, you should not use it for anything that may be an attempt to enforce your will on another's life. No matter how good your intent may be, you should not use Anger Magic for anything you have not thought through completely. Nor should you use it for anything that goes against your ethics.

I don't think I can control my anger, why can't I just ignore it?

Denial of one's anger can build up and explode (or implode) in a myriad of ways. You may feel smothered or attacked. You may feel listless and rundown. Unreleased anger causes tension and frustration. Tension can wreak havoc on the body. You may find yourself clenching your jaw or grinding your teeth. You may notice a haggard appearance and the developing of frown lines. You may experience weight fluctuations. Then there are larger health risks too.

To not acknowledge, and therefore validate, anger makes for high levels of frustration. Anger is necessary and vital. You cannot have light without dark, and you cannot have happiness without anger.

Dealing with your anger is not dangerous, ignoring it is. You run the risk of it bursting out wild of its own accord. Instead of empowering you, anger can demean you if not released properly. Think of it this way: During a game of billiards you can bang the balls as hard as you wish and shoot them in rapid succession. Every now and again, you may be lucky enough to sink one. Nevertheless, if you take your time, line up your shots correctly, and use precision and control when shooting, you will sink a lot more balls.

But how can I control my anger? It always catches me off guard!

There are many ways to control anger and also to store it for energy reserves that you may make use of at a later time, when you are better prepared.

To develop your control, the most important thing you can do is to follow the exercises in this book daily. This will give you a clearer view of what exactly is making you angry and how you can use your anger productively.

What are the critical points of working with anger?

1. *Focus:* Your focus must be clear and maintained. Working with angry energy is not easy—it takes work. You must keep control at all times. Because of this, I recommend working with Anger Magic only in a sacred circle, so that it is not released until you are sure it is ready to be released. Once the energy has been transformed, the circle will no longer be necessary, but as the work begins with anger in a raw state, the circle is a safety precaution.

2. *Volatility:* Anger is a very volatile emotion, associated with chaos. Because of this, I do not recommend using it for pulling things to you, unless you neutralize it first. Ideally, you should harness it and use it to rid yourself of harmful energies.

3. *Overpowering:* This has been brought up to me time and again. Fear that working with anger may overwhelm you and that you may not be able to control it is exactly that—a fear. Would you rather that you control your anger or vice versa? Face it, embrace it, and use it. It is not going to just go away. Giving in to this fear is acceptance that one of your emotions holds more power than you do, and how is that possible when it is yours?

What about karma? How can I be sure of avoiding rebound?

The key step to avoiding karmic rebound lies in where you direct the energy.

Using Anger Magic to improve your own circumstances or life is the best way to avoid any sort of karmic backlash. Once you attempt to involve another person or change his or her circumstances, you are inviting karmic retribution. However, it need not be assumed that this will be a negative consequence. If you stopped an incident of abuse, the backlash related to it would be of a positive nature. Karmic backlash is all in the individual's perception.

Is it ethical to use anger for destruction?

Yes, but using anger for destruction can be devastating if not done correctly. Ideally, this type of magic should only be used on yourself.

You cannot, no matter how much you may wish to, use Anger Magic to destroy anything in anyone else's life, even for healing purposes, without an invitation for rebound. However, here again, it is the circumstances that determine whether that rebound will be negative or positive.

Can anger be tamed enough for true transformation?

Yes, although it takes considerable time and effort. There are no shortcuts or quick fixes when it comes to the transformation process. It is vital that you follow each step.

There are several processes to accomplish the transformation; all are safe and effective. Once your mind is in the right place, the transformations are easy to perform. The hard part is usually caused by the human ego.

Can I use anger to manifest?

Absolutely! The most certain way is transforming anger into raw energy, but anger in and of itself may be used to manifest certain desires, like privacy or shielding.

Can I use anger to create?

Yes, in fact anger is a powerful creative force. Tapping into it can be a boon for artists and creative persons.

In a creative capacity, transformation is not required, as the act of creating works as a purgative.

If you create something you wish to keep, sell, or give away, I recommend a simple cleansing of the item, to remove any negative traces that may be left behind.

What about cursing? Can I use anger for that?

Yes, you can. I am not going to teach you how to curse people, however, as I believe such behavior goes against the soul's purpose in this life, and that you may ultimately harm yourself by such an action in the long run.

I encourage control of anger, and if you are in such a state of rage that you don't care what harm you bring to others via a curse, then you are not in control. If you aren't in charge, then your spell will not work anyway, so why bother?

Certain instances may call for retribution—as a form of justice. In such a case, if you are willing to face all the consequences, then you must follow your heart. Even so, you must be in control of your anger to obtain the desired effect.

How can you tell the difference between righteous anger and petty anger? Which one is correct for magical use?

Anger stems from many things—jealousy, for instance—but once transformed it does not matter. You may use either type.

If you are certain that your anger is righteous, then you may proceed with spells that are in line with raw anger use. A "No More Gossip" spell, for example.

Often, in a case involving righteous anger, the spell will pack more of a punch than the raw energy after a transformation could.

Deciding the type of anger you are dealing with comes from a thorough examination of the problem and the emotions elicited.

Before using righteous anger, you must study your motives carefully as well as the possible consequences. Jumping the gun on this can ruin any right you have to righteous anger and the results could be catastrophic.

What are some examples of righteous anger?

Righteous anger is a healthy type of anger that stems from an obvious wrong. Fury at having been abused, for example. There are varying degrees of righteous anger. Having been embarrassed in a meeting by inappropriate remarks directed at you by coworkers, may not be on the same level as abuse, but the anger evoked is righteous nevertheless.

Simply stated, if you could remove yourself from the equation, and imagine the same thing happening to another person, would you still be angry on his behalf? Then the anger is righteous.

What about petty anger?

Petty anger is harder to define, but basically, if it would not be a big deal to another person, it is a good idea to figure out why the happenstance is important to you. Your anger is valid either way, but if you are angry because the cute waitress flirted with your boyfriend—that's petty anger.

Petty anger stems from our individual perception of the world. It thrives in our own reality. However, in order for it to become useful magically, it should first be transformed into raw energy. But petty anger is tricky—if we are not careful we can demean ourselves by expressing it and harm our overall self-image. Petty anger is often not true anger at all, but a mask for insecurity. However, petty anger can also be an inner warning that something just is not right. Determining what you are really feeling requires a thorough examination of the facts.

Petty anger is always present for a reason; it exists to make you look a bit deeper into the situation and find a suitable resolution. In the case of the cute waitress, it could be that the woman needs to deal with insecurity issues of her own, or it could be a warning that her present relationship is not suitable for her. It might be a "wake up" signal to alert you to the fact that it may be time to reevaluate a few things. Petty anger is not actually "petty"; it is simply highly individualized.

How can I be sure the transformation process is complete?

This works on a case-by-case basis. You will know because you will feel it. Sometimes you may be moved to another emotion altogether, such as sadness or confusion.

When the anger is transformed completely, you will feel empty and possibly weak.

What is a proper release?

A proper release will have the following three key elements:

1. *Satisfaction:* After a proper release of anger you should feel a definite surge of satisfaction.

2. *Control:* During a proper release, you, not the anger, are in complete control.

3. *Empowerment:* This is your confidence kicking in. Acceptance of anger and releasing it in a healthy manner builds confidence.

Don't fall into the foul language trap! This is an excellent example of an improper release. You are not reaping any benefits from this! Rather, you are showing yourself, and whoever may be watching, that you are not prepared to handle your anger as an adult and in a productive manner.

Will I attract negative entities to me by using anger in a circle?

No. A circle is necessary to hold the anger until the transformation is complete.

While working magically with anger, the circle serves several purposes. This circle contains the energy until you are ready to release it; it guards you and your magic from contamination by any negative entities that may already be present. It also forms a barrier between places where your anger may or may not go.

You will define this barrier during the casting of the circle as a failsafe. It can be a simple verbal announcement of limitations you are placing on the energy, such as, "The energy contained by this circle, upon release, may not stray into my family life, love life, or worklife." When assigning this task to your circle, it is appropriate to consider parallel (similar) areas of the spell's goal so that you will know which area of your life is at risk for possible side effects, and which to safeguard.

The deities in this book are a little on the dark side, are you sure this is not black magic?

Yes, I am sure. The dark exists for a reason, as does the light. The buzzards are perceived as dark creatures, feeding from the carcasses of the dead. Nevertheless, they are necessary as scavengers and without them disease would run rampant.

The myths presented here, while they may appear a bit dark, can teach us about the true nature of anger—such as which things to avoid and which to embrace, as well as the differences between righteous anger and petty anger. Dark or not, the deities I will discuss later on directly relate to our understanding of anger.

Using Anger for Justice Work

Justice work is used in an attempt to restore balance to an off-kilter universe. This condition may have come about because someone enacted a vicious attack upon our body, soul, or mind; or it may be that taking action is required against one who is a threat to others. Many times when we are victimized we are left with little to no recourse. Calling upon the divine to restore balance is partaking in justice magic.

Justice follows the rule of tit for tat. Anger is a perfect motivator for justice work, providing you follow a few rules and guidelines about justice work in general.

The most important thing in justice work is determining whether or not it is something you can handle. Divinity has instilled within some of us, a strong sense of fairness. Such people are preordained for justice work. If you are not certain that you are one of them, do not try justice work. Even when angry you must be fair to avoid harm to yourself via karmic payback. It is not a good idea to ask that the person suffers any more than the victim has. Remember tit for tat and ask only that they suffer the same amount.

This type of work is not something you can run into blindly or cast a spell for personal reasons just this once. Justice work is a calling, a path, and if you tread it, know that it will revisit you. It completes a full circle, so an action you stimulate will return to— and end with—you.

Anger Magic and justice works have this in common: neither is for the dabbler. They are not about violence. Instead, we seek control over anger and once that control is achieved, we will have stronger magical skills. Violence is a sign of weakness. Violence to another harms us all, as we are all part of one whole.

Violence does have a connection to anger, but it is only through an immature response pattern. The purpose of working with anger is to change our responses and quash violent tendencies.

Before considering a justice working, use this quiz to help you determine if using this energy, for the purpose in mind, would be beneficial to you. The quiz works on a case-by-case basis and it is a good idea to use it each time before you attempt angry justice.

Answer all the following questions, in detail, on a separate sheet of paper.

1. How confident do you feel about the possible outcome of this working?
2. Have you reconsidered this decision at all?
3. Are you focused on the goal?
4. Is this working for you only?
5. Could you put this working off for thirty days and still feel as strongly about it as you do now?
6. Why are you doing this?
7. Would you recommend this route to your closest friend?
8. Have you considered karmic consequence?
9. Can you handle this working?
10. Could this working bring harm to innocent parties?

Wait a day. Then, answer the questions again. Compare the answers; are they identical (in terms of the idea, not the actual wording)? Do you still hold firm to the concept of this working? If the answers to these two questions are yes, then your reasons must be pretty stern stuff. Please pay particular attention to question 5. A thirty-day building-up or cooling-off period can bring about many changes. If it is at all possible to wait thirty days before proceeding, it will be to your benefit to do so.

Could I have a predestination to handle anger in a certain manner?

Your astrological sign may be a determining factor in how you handle anger initially. You could be born with a predisposition to handle it a certain way. While each sign has many wonderful qualities, this section deals only with tendencies regarding anger. It is a general overview that does not take into account your moon sign, which has just as much to do with emotional processes as does your sun sign, and it is meant to help you identify possible problem areas.

Aquarius: Aquarians can be wishy-washy. Their moods change with the wind. When angered, Aquarians can become nasty and cause intentional harm through words and deeds; five seconds later, they don't understand why anyone is mad at them.

Libra: Libras have a strong tendency to run from arguments and later stew in their anger. They waffle on decisions and have a hard time reaching conclusions. Some have tendencies to manipulate situations. Often they assign blame to others.

Gemini: Gemini folks can handle the anger of others very well. Often they can see clearly on the surface of things and help others navigate around a problem. However, they can also turn a blind eye to pressing issues and can rarely see through to the heart of the matter. When it comes to their own anger, Geminis are prone to hold grudges.

Sagittarius: Sagittarians have a tendency to open their mouths before thinking the situation through. They are reckless and impulsive. Sagittarius folks tend to erupt into tantrums, but the tantrums are usually over with quickly.

Leo: The key word for Leo folk is *pushy*! They tend to want to control the actions of others but are rarely successful in controlling their own. Leos are hotheaded and highly temperamental.

Aries: People born under the sign of Aries must be especially careful to avoid rash actions and reactions. Often they are prone to violent fits of temper and later regret their actions. Aries folk should slow down when dealing with anger and allow for all facets of the situation to show before deciding upon action. Aries also tend to be controlling individuals.

Scorpio: Scorpio folk are well known problem solvers. When it comes to the anger of others, Scorpios are astute observers. Their own anger tends to be violent. They easily see below the surface into the heart of the matter and are apt to be judgmental. They hold grudges indefinitely.

Taurus: Taurus has a special battle with anger—jealousy, which is often the root of their temperamental behavior. Once convinced of something, a Taurus will not change his mind. They also hold on to grudges.

Capricorn: Capricorns are disciplined, patient, and methodical. When anger gets through to Capricorns, they are capable of blind hatred. Capricorns often seek to remove or destroy the object of their anger and will most likely hold grudges. However, they usually think the situation through before acting.

Virgo: Virgo folk tend to bitch and moan often. They cannot resist the urge to criticize and complain. Virgos also tend to worry. While they pay attention to the smallest detail, they often miss the bigger picture entirely.

Pisces: Pisces incline to be very laid back and are slow to anger. However, once roused their anger runs hot. An angry Pisces isn't pretty and will hold a grudge indefinitely. The problem for Pisces is usually deciding if the situation is worthy of action. They tend to overthink the emotional process and may be seen as emotionally cold. Rarely are they rash in their decisions.

Cancer: Cancers tend to take on the anger of others. Threats to their safety, or the safety of those they love, bring out their violent streak. They are moody by nature and quick to change from happiness to anger to depression.

Any predisposition to anger can be retrained. Once you recognize your problem areas it is usually easy to make a conscious effort to change them.

Now that we have dealt with all of the pesky little details and gotten them out of the way, what say we go make some magic?

2. Who's in Charge?

When dealing with anger, the most commonly expressed concern is the control issue. Most people think that anger is so primitive it must be a separate part of them. They seem to think that anger has a mind of its own and does whatever it wants. This is not true. Your anger belongs to you. It is whatever you wish it to be; you simply have to take charge of it.

Adults sometimes allow their anger to rule their actions and actually throw things, cry, jump up and down, and scream obscenities. Some even punch concrete walls. I have watched as friends destroyed their own property in a fury. These are the same adults who ask how you can control your anger. My answer to them is simple, how can you *not*?

A case in point concerns a young mother and her child in line ahead of me at the grocery store a few days ago. The child appeared to be about four years old, and the mother was pushing a cart full of groceries. It was obvious the young mother was having a bad day. Her face was contorted in a frown and her little girl was whining. The mother was struggling to empty the contents of the cart onto the store's counter so they could be rung up on the cash register for purchase. It was slow going.

When the clerk finally finished ringing her up and pressed the total key the shopper handed her a one-inch stack of coupons. The clerk sighed wearily and the shopper just exploded. She started yelling at the clerk and accused her of not liking coupon shoppers. She never even realized that by doing so she was teaching her daughter the same bad control habits (not to mention rudeness).

The eyes of the clerk, who was also having a bad day, welled up with tears and her chin began to wiggle, as it so often does before a person cries. It seems that the clerk had sighed because her boyfriend—who had broken up with her that very morning—had just walked in the store. I ask you, which one of the two ladies had a right to be angry?

If you guessed the clerk, you are only half right. They both did. However, the mother had no right to attack the poor clerk with her anger. If she had calmly asked the cashier if there was a problem, she would have found there was not. The point is that the mother's anger was valid and real, but completely misdirected and out of control. If the equivalent were to happen in a magical setting it would be disastrous. As it is, in everyday life, the young mother now has to reap what she has sown. Everything comes full circle, and her day would most likely get even more frustrating. Misplaced anger may be directed at her, making her day even worse.

No one can take your anger from you; you have to give it away. Each and every time you do that, you risk having it turn and fly right back at you. Anger is powerful: why would you want to give your power away? Especially when it can be used against you.

Many give their anger away by using foul language toward another, or refusing to speak at all. For some the very vibration of anger radiates from them and can be felt by others. Then there are those who are moved to acts of violence. These people are not in charge of their emotions.

If I were to tease you and provoke you to the point that you scream profanities at me, who's in charge of your anger now? I am, that's who. If after doing so, I sit there just looking at you as if you were nuts, you may begin to turn red and become embarrassed. Doubt follows closely on the heels of anger. If you find yourself wondering whether you were overreacting, it is a sure sign that you were just attacked by your own emotion. Even worse is the realization that you allowed me to orchestrate the whole incident.

There are certain types of people who think it's funny to provoke anger in others; they feed off doing so. Such people are called *psychic vampires*. You have to watch closely for psychic vampires, they can manipulate your emotions before you know what happened and by doing so, they obtain control of you in a very real sense.

When you allow a psy-vamp to manipulate you, you are giving him everything he needs to make his behavior into a continuing habit. You are granting control over something that is uniquely yours and a very part of your soul. If he can take it, why wouldn't he?

The psychic vampire often appears lonely and needy for friendship. Once established as his friend, however, you quickly realize that friendship is a one-way street. If you opt to share a bit of yourself, he will turn the tables on you and twist your words until you doubt yourself as much as he doubts himself. It is from instilling you with self-doubt that psy-vamps draw their strength. From that point, the psychic vampire becomes your worst enemy and yet will often masquerade as your closest friend. The old adage, "misery loves company" perfectly defines the psychic vampire.

Psychic vampires are full of self-doubt and seek to raise themselves to what they see as a more desirable level by lowering everyone else. They wish only to be seen as above others when we are all, in fact, equal. They count on the ability to do a job so thoroughly deceptive that no one will ever see through it. The rationale is if other people feel worse about their lives, then the psy-vamp can feel better about his own. Therefore, he will try to paint everything in a negative light for everyone else.

All is comparison for the psy-vamp. In order for his life to sparkle, in his own perception, yours must be seen as dull or dim. If he can convince you that he has a better life than you do, he rationalizes that this must be so.

All too often when dealing with a psy-vamp, once you give away your power by losing your temper, you never get it back. That bit of energy now belongs to him and will live on in his memory indefinitely. The person who took your anger frequently loses respect for you. He loses respect because of the simple fact that you could not control yourself, even if he deliberately provoked you. Console yourself with the knowledge that in the case of the psy-vamp, he had barely any respect for you in the first place.

Then there is also—lights, camera, and drama. Chances are you know one or two of the people I am speaking about. We have all seen or know drama queens. They are the siblings of the psy-vamp. Their methods are different but the effects are the same. It seems nothing can ever go right in their lives for very long. Every day yields a new soap-opera event; they are always under attack from someone or something. Such is a day in the life of a drama queen.

The drama queen often needs to have an enemy to feel complete. In order for her to make herself out to be an innocent victim, there must be an evil villain. Often, she chooses her closest friend to play the villain role; sometimes she may choose a person she doesn't know well enough to consider an acquaintance, much less an enemy.

The drama queen often lives in a sick world where fantasies become realities. Any remark that does not suit her, even a simple disagreement, and she thinks the person who does not agree with her is "out to get her." She is always broke and always sick. No one loves her (at least in her mind). She has a tendency to make cryptic comments and suicidal remarks.

The most unfortunate behavior exhibited by many drama queen Witches is a predisposition to curse or otherwise attack magically. It is a sad statement indeed that such still goes on in this day and time.

Two women I know were recently attacked by a drama queen Witch. The first was attacked with stabbing pains in her head. It was quick. She felt the presence of the attacker and she felt the needle sliding into her head. It hurt. She took action. She stopped the needle and began pushing it back at the attacker, twice as hard and twice as long. When she found she was actually enjoying hurting the attacker and felt the attacker start to cry, she stopped.

Immediately she held an impromptu ritual and burned every connection she had to the attacker. She called upon her goddess and the winds of change and blew the attacker out of her life forever. A short while later she spoke to the second woman and found the exact same type of attack had occurred, only this time it was not directed at the woman. It had been focused on her family. The second woman took action too. She held a ritual and called a permanent halt to any vibrations sent from the attacker. Both of them stopped the attacks by calling upon the force of anger.

The saddest part of all is that in this case the drama queen did not understand anything other than being "slapped back." You can try to heal a drama queen, but often she will only continue to attack. This can be very confusing for the young Witch and for those who don't believe curses have the potential to affect you if you do not believe in them. Yes, they can, do, and will. Like it or not, curses do exist—and their potential for harm is great. In this day and age of discarding a belief that doesn't suit you personally, even though it fits and makes sense, you can open yourself up for real pain. You must know how to fight fire with fire.

Most drama queens are easily identified. A few are sneaky and hide their dramatic flair until you are sucked into their world and they can be assured you will agree that any problem is simply a dramatic event.

To avoid allowing psy-vamps, drama queens, and others to manipulate your emotions, when dealing with other people each time you feel as if you are being baited into losing your temper, ask yourself what you would do if the person baiting you were your boss, your mother, or a judge in court? What would you say then? How can you respond and not lose ownership of something so valuable as your own emotion? The answer to that is simple as well; remove the anger from the equation before responding. Store it and deal with it later when you can make use of it in a positive manner. Better yet, use it to build a powerful shield, blocking any manipulators from affecting you. The only exception to this strategy is during an attack, when it is best to act immediately and shield yourself from damage.

Once you allow someone else to control your anger, you are in effect giving him or her ammunition to destroy a part of your life. This happens frequently in couple situations after a nasty breakup. The parties find it hard—and sometimes even think it impossible—to move on. Anger is a natural part of the grieving process but the process should not stop there. If one partner didn't deserve to be with the other in the first place, why on Earth should either deserve to control such a large part of the other's energy?

If your boss is yelling at you because of a simple goof and you are angry about it, you can use a harnessing method to contain the energy for now. Later you can take the time to examine it and determine if your anger was righteous or petty, and decide what you would like to do with the energy. There is no need to waste it; save it.

I often see motorists who are angry at being cut off or delayed, using that interference as an excuse to vent a little anger. They sometimes stick their heads out of the vehicle windows and shout obscenities or make faces and honk the horn constantly. They never stop to think about the energy exchange that just happened. I am sure they feel their confidence ebb a bit and their self-respect drop a notch, even if they do not realize it at first. One thing is certain; their anger is out there for the taking.

Have you ever flipped someone off in traffic? Then you know what I mean: You have given them a tool to make a fool out of you, and by doing so, you have made a fool out of yourself. Would you go up to the person you flipped off and hand them a pint of your blood for cutting you off? Or your car keys? You may as well, because what you are giving them when you give them your anger is as powerful and valuable as either of those. With Anger Magic, the control must be complete. You cannot just give it away.

Often when we are angry, blame is assigned to others. People do not want to own their anger. Phrases like "She made me mad" assign blame to another person for the solicitation of your emotional response, the equivalent of saying you never had control in the first place. We also transfer ownership of our emotions by reacting instead of acting, and later try to excuse ourselves by blaming others.

Am I saying that you can no longer vent to rid yourself of the excess? No, I am saying you can learn new ways of venting that will retain your rightful ownership of your emotions.

One of the most harmful things I have seen people do is use bad judgment about where they choose to vent. Sarah vents to a friend about her lazy husband, for example, hoping to feel better about the situation. What usually happens instead is the friend no longer has any respect for the husband, and may lose respect for Sarah as well. Why? Sarah just told her she does not have to respect them. By venting to her friend, she diminished herself and her husband in her friend's eyes. This is the same man her friend found delightful at dinner last week. Because she liked him, if she agrees with Sarah she is invalidating her ability to judge. If she disagrees, an argument could ensue and she might be accused of undermining her friend. She is unsure of how to respond, and on some level finds Sarah a bit shallow. She most likely feels attacked by this sort of venting—because there is no correct response. She probably does not want ownership of the anger presented to her and in self-defense may withdraw emotionally from Sarah. Sarah may find herself unconsciously defending a husband who has not been attacked by anyone other than herself. This is a defense mechanism set in motion by knowing—on some level—that she gave ownership of her anger at her husband to her friend and may now be attacked with it or by it. And the husband is an innocent victim of his wife's verbal lashing. This type of venting is almost a rehearsal for out-of-control anger. The aggressiveness of it will grow. Who was served by this? No one; everyone involved loses.

So, how can you vent safely? Choose your outlet consciously, at a time when you are not angry, and decide which method of dealing with anger would work best for you. Do the exercises and meditations in this book faithfully, until you can react calmly in any situation. Retrain your response patterns. Finally, give yourself and your friends a break. You are not going to be perfect no matter how hard you try, but you will always be you, which in itself is perfect. In the case of your friends, it's not that they don't care, but that uncontrolled venting places them in a very tough spot.

I frequently hear from people congratulating themselves for *not* being in control of their own actions. They say things like, "I wanted to kill him, but I was good. I only assaulted him instead." They try to interpret their action to fit into their view of themselves as truly in charge, when the reality is far different. To be in complete control, one would not give in to one's urges until after an *appropriate* course of action had been determined. Giving in to urges without thought is like settling for a crumb instead of a whole piece of cake. Problems arise when the craving for cake has not been completely satisfied, and the piece of cake is still right in front of you. The preceding helps explain why transferring emotion into a storage facility before taking action is always your best bet.

The only times you can "assault" someone and still be in control is if doing so is in self-defense, or as a protective measure for your family. Both of these situations must be marked by a direct threat of harm. However, you may have ethical entanglements to deal with on assault issues and should always follow your own heart. I do not recommend assault, but I do recommend restraining the aggressor from harming anyone.

The nature of anger is very confusing and we often don't know where it comes from. We make use of it immediately upon feeling it, and this is how we lose control of it. Angry actions must be deliberate and precise. Precision requires knowledge and detailed introspection. Once you know every detail about that little bundle of emotion, you can use it however you wish.

Here are a few quick techniques to diffuse reactions so that you may save your anger for future use:

Sprinkle yourself with water.
Dip your right hand in a shallow dish of water.
Drink a glass of water.
Keep a crystal, for storage purposes, and hold it tight in your right hand.
Touch a plant or dirt.
Spray lavender-scented air spray.
Grab a paper bag and breathe your anger into it.
Put on a hat.
Carry something black and transfer the anger to it.
Write it down.
Visualize a small dragon on your left shoulder eating your anger. When using this method keep in mind the dragon will breathe your anger back to you as fire when you ask for it.

Important note: Utilizing these techniques will diminish the power of the anger, and to put it to use it must be called out in full force again. Be very careful that you do not banish the anger entirely; rather store it for later.

3. Sticky Ethics

Life is an individual journey. You are born into your body alone and you will die alone. It makes sense that the ethics you set must be tailored to suit you. No one else can tell you what feels right to your soul. When it comes to setting your ethics in Anger Magic, you must really look hard at each individual situation. The trick to making wise choices is often to first take the anger out of the equation. That is not always so easy to do. The ability to do it varies widely from person to person, based on personal experience of the subject matter.

You will notice I have not provided an answer for all of the following scenarios. That is because I can't. You must make the choices on your own. The answers I *have* provided are not examples of my own ethics; rather, they are alternative choices and magical facts that you should be aware of.

Ethics should never be black and white; things are rarely so simple. A blanket code of *never lie*, for example, can blow up in your face if telling the "whole truth" will hurt beyond repair, and there is no redeeming reason to do so. Every situation is composed of many shades of gray. For that reason, I do not recommend devising a blanket code of ethics. I encourage examining each situation independently and deciding upon the best course of action individually.

Keeping an open mind allows you the freedom to find alternate choices that would not apply if you maintained a blanket position. An automatic response pattern cheats every soul involved.

The following scenarios are meant to help you define and identify with free-thinking ethics and the formation of creative solutions.

Scenario One: A rapist is torturing and raping innocent women in your neighborhood. What can you do?

Your options, to name a few, are concentrate on protection for the neighborhood, focus on having him caught, bind him to prevent it from happening to anyone else, or heal him of the sickness that causes him to rape. If you work for protecting the neighborhood, he may roam freely on to other areas and continue his crimes. If you bind him, you run a big karmic risk for imposing your will on another person. If you focus on having him caught, he may have to rape again in order for that to happen. If you heal him, your energies may become entangled with his and you may be inviting negative karma to visit you from assuming a responsibility for his future actions. There are issues with each choice and no easy way out; it all comes down to how you see it.

Once you think you know the proper solution, ask yourself if the choice would change if it were your daughter, mother, or even you who had been raped. Ask yourself, If you choose to work toward having him captured and he must rape again for that to happen, will it be your fault for not binding him and preventing it? Is it your responsibility to do so? Is it your responsibility to do anything? Is it worth the karmic risk to you to do something about it or would you face larger consequences by opting out? It's a very sticky situation and could be viewed as damned-if-you-do and damned-if-you-don't.

Is there a magical solution with no threat of harm to yourself or others? Yes, but you don't get to choose it. If you feel it goes against your ethics to take an active position, you would be better served if you ask divinity to step in and show you the path you are to follow. For that I recommend you conjure a fire circle and call forth Kali-Ma. A ritual in chapter 27 details how to do this. When attempting to make a decision concerning justice through magic, do not forget to define your barriers (more on barriers can be found in chapter 8). When it comes to carrying out the plan Kali has for you, research your weak spots and barricade them as well.

Scenario Two: Someone you know and love is dying of cancer. You are angry and wish to cast a spell of destruction on the cancer cells for hurting this person. Can you heal using a method of destruction?

I'm sorry, but no. No matter how much you may wish to, the risk is great to you and greater still to the poor cancer victim. Your anger at the cancer is yours; the most you can hope for magically is that the victim is angry enough at the cancer to perform the needed magic. Maybe she will wish to heal herself. You are allowed to try to heal yourself, and anger is a healing energy. However, to use a destruction spell on a living body is inviting death and is therefore too risky. In addition, the power of raw angry energy is hot. It could easily burn the victim or you. You should never "point" it at a living thing because of the damage you could inflict on both it and on yourself. Living things often have a natural shielding and the possibility of the destruction mirroring back to you is very real.

Anger is not suitable for physical healing. Our minds and soul can handle it, our bodies cannot. When healing someone's body you need the gentle touch of love. When healing the soul, however, anger is often the perfect catalyst.

The polarity between love and anger is interesting. Anger is considered the shadow side of love, and yet anger is the emotion that drives the soul to grow. Love stagnates and gives one a contentment to remain in the moment, while anger forces change. How you use it determines whether that change is an improvement.

Having said that, you may easily attempt to bind the cancer. This does not heal, but it may stop the progression a bit. You should transform the anger first, back into raw energy, to avoid unintended harm.

An even better solution would be to store the transformed energy in a crystal and place it beside the person's bed within her reach. If she needs an energy boost, she can pick up the stone and hold it, absorbing its energy that way. The body is miraculous and works consistently to try to heal itself. Adding a little energy boost is not only ethical but also thoughtful and giving. By performing this action you are inviting the full circle of caring and friendship to return to you, which is a positive use for anger and most certainly an action, not a reaction.

Scenario Three: A close friend attempts suicide and fails. You feel he may try again as soon as he can, and you are angry. You may be angry with your friend or the situation. What do you do?

Here again, this is a choice only you can make. You can ignore your pain and focus on support for your friend. However, you must eventually deal with your emotions. Before you attempt any sort of magical solution with anger of this type, it is critical to first determine the stem of the anger. A few hard questions to ask yourself are: Are you angry because your friend would be leaving you behind? Are you angry because he may want to die and leave you? If so, isn't it selfish to expect him to continue on in misery just for you?

If you have asked yourself these questions and still want to carry onward with an action, the answer to the risk-free question is yes, provided that the magical action is directed at the person's situation, not at him. You may wish to bind his actions, thus removing the threat of his harming himself. You may employ protective magic. But can you utilize your anger, in a magically risk-free manner?

You can, but to do that you run a risk to yourself mentally, not to mention karmically. You run those risks because you have to put yourself completely in his shoes. Entering the depths of despair is easy; getting out is another matter entirely. I do not recommend placing yourself in his shoes so squarely, but it can be done.

The safest way to do it is to swallow the anger and see it inside your belly. Now, visualize yourself as a great fire-breathing dragon, the seed of anger in your belly is the source of your fire. Perform the dark-side-of-life tarot ritual in chapter 27.

If you choose this road, design a good cleansing and purification ritual so that you can rid yourself of the pain from the other person's feelings. The normal cleansing exercises may not be strong or thorough enough.

Once you have performed the ritual, you will understand the situation of your friend a bit more and then may wish to use magical work to diminish the negative influences around him. But be very careful not to remove the influences entirely, since they are a part of who the person is and you have no right to remove them altogether. Remember that anything you do will have a full-circle effect and come back to you.

A more suitable alternative is to add a bright spot in each area. For example, if the main cause of despair is love, add a new possibility and a bit of hope to the person's outlook. Do so only in small doses or you could wind up with an accidental setup for failure, thus unintentionally increasing the depth of his despair.

The karmic consequence of such work is severe. Even though you may do it with the very best of intentions, you are stepping over boundaries and entering his private universe. You are invading the privacy of his mind and soul—there is no way you can avoid a backlash. In this case your anger could become your friend's, the same way that you are taking on his feelings to understand him. The anger he assumes may be directed at you, so if you don't wish to be attacked by your own anger do not attempt the ritual. More-over, be aware that such an invasion, regardless of its purpose, could be seen by him as grounds for ending your friendship.

The bright spot in this is that anger may be just what this person needs to climb out of the depression and begin healing.

Anger may help him to begin the process of self-defense. While you may lose him as a friend, you may help him to continue with his life. As with all things, there is a give and take and everything comes full circle. Make sure to set your barriers concerning your own privacy before proceeding and do so only with the understanding that while you are opening his mind to you, your mind is equally open to him.

Of course, that is only one way of approaching the situation from a magical standpoint. If you are practicing free-thinking ethics you should see many more choices open to you. Think it through and choose the one you feel is best.

Scenario Four: Someone has attempted to place a curse on you. What do you do, and can you use Anger Magic as a curative?

The power of anger is immense. In this case, you are working with two angry forces, yours and theirs. Since the person who has attempted this curse is so willing to hand over all this power—and in such a destructive way—you may manipulate it how you like. Your first step should be to construct a shield of protection with your own anger. Then you may wish to freeze the curser's anger or write it down and erase it. You can bury it or allow it to thrive in a useful environment. By "useful environment," I mean possibly employed as a guardian. You can store it in a statue and allow it to look over your garden as a weed watcher, for instance. You may even throw it away.

If you choose employment, you will probably have to transform the anger into a protector and destroy the attack mode it is in. This can be a difficult and lengthy process, but it need not be. In chapter 27 I have provided simple, easy-to-perform methods to allow for the transformation of anger sent to you by others. Most important—these methods work.

One way—my personal favorite—to use an employment method without transformation is in a greenhouse setting. If you are growing a particularly nasty herb, you may feed it the anger. It is important to note that the resulting plant will be extremely poisonous and should be used only in a curse or banishing situation, but it will pack a powerful magical punch. As a protective measure, I would keep this plant quarantined from the rest of the greenhouse. You may also want to enchant the pot to assure no possibility of cross contamination.

You should also enclose this plant in an iron cage, to keep fairies away. You do not want them attracted to it and feeding from its energies. For the fairies' protection, be sure to declare verbally that it is your wish they do not come near it. It would also be appropriate to leave distant offerings such as bowls of milk and honey, somewhere distant from this plant, preferably near a foxglove that you have planted for their pleasure.

To feed a plant anger, poke a small hole in each end of an egg and blow out the contents into a small bowl. You may use the empty shell as a vessel to contain the anger received. Light a black candle to absorb the angry energy. After the candle is burned to the halfway point, begin to drip the wax into the shell. Three drops, no more. Allow the shell to sit beside the candle while the candle continues to burn itself out. Know that the shell is now absorbing the energy. Once the candle burns out completely, crush the shell into a fine powder and bury it in the dirt of your chosen plant. Or you may wish to bury the eggshell whole and allow the roots to crush it as the plant grows.

Alternatively, you may wish to send the anger back to its home. A simple mirror spell will take care of that for you. Moreover, if bad karma is reaped it will not be yours. If, however, you did wrong this person first you may wish to hold on to the anger in a statue or stone as a reminder for a while. It may be painful for you, but anger stimulates growth no matter who sends it your way. Allowing and accepting the anger of others actually empowers you in the long run.

Concerning curses: As practicing Witches, we work to attain a certain level of openness with universal vibrations. Therefore, entertaining curses at long length in our minds has the potential to work as an attractant. By allowing the thought to form, it exists. If we feed it with emotion, a cursed-like state may ensue in our own lives through a subconscious manifestation of what we may secretly desire for others. Many times, we are willing to face the consequences of our actions, and if you consciously decide to curse someone, you must follow your own heart. However, guard yourself against cursing your own life accidentally by dwelling on the wrongs done to you. Be aware and mindful of your thought forms.

Just as each scenario was not black and white, neither are the choices of available response. The choices I presented are merely the tip of the iceberg. The key to using Anger Magic responsibly is thinking it through. Perform actions that you will not mind having come full circle back to you. Accept the anger and decide what it's best suited for. When in doubt, wait it out!

4. Karma vs. The Rule of Three

Some folks believe in a threefold to tenfold return for every action we perform. Others believe in a simpler system: an action equals a reaction.

While either belief can be seen as one spiritual aspect of a path, for this discussion we will look harder at the magical properties and facts that relate specifically to Anger Magic. Belief in a return law is almost universal. When multiplied it can take on a property reminiscent of dogma. The Wiccan Rede cites a threefold return. This is sometimes taken to mean a return on the action performed in a spiritual, emotional, and physical sense instead of a magnification three times over.

For Anger Magic, we assume the position of full circle, meaning everything that goes around, comes back around. The full-circle effect, as explained here, should not be seen as an attempt to set your ethics for you. It is simply a clarification of how vibrations travel and what the energy is appropriate for.

If your boss had a bad day and called you a dork, and you are angry, which of the following would you do?

a. Perform an action—leave the room.

b. Perform a reaction—yell a name back.

c. Perform an inaction—stand there looking at him and do nothing. Nothing to warn him off, nothing at all.

Of those three examples, which one *could* have a positive effect?

Every action, reaction, or inaction you take (or don't take) is a conscious choice and will return to you. If you take action, it will return as action. If you choose inaction, it will return as inaction. Not understanding that inaction itself *is* an action, in and of itself, is a common mistake. Not realizing that choosing a passive role returns, a person may find herself stuck in a situation she feels she can't do anything about. She may find herself in need of help that does not come.

I often hear the statement, "I didn't even *do* anything!" The fact that the speaker did not do anything has nothing to do with what—if any—action may be required. People assume passivity allows one to bow out of a situation; it does not. In fact, passivity often borders on denial. By not doing anything, you are inviting a full circle of inaction to return to you. In that manner, inaction *is* an action. Having the attitude of "I didn't do anything" is an attempt to excuse yourself *from* doing anything. There is none of that in Anger Magic.

If you are not careful, inaction can mean that you give up your rights. Would you allow your best friend or teenaged child to become drug addicted by inaction? If you knew they were using drugs and did nothing to educate them, or help them deal with it, you would be partially responsible for allowing it. There is a point, and the point is determined individually, where we must take on a responsibility for others and we must always do so for ourselves. Telling yourself that something is not your problem will not cut it in Anger Magic. When I speak of action in Anger Magic, I mean taking steps or doing something to change a situation. These steps can be taken in the physical or the astral realms.

There will be times when inaction (passivity) is appropriate. Times when, as a friend, you are needed just to listen and comfort. However, you should never lose sight of the full-circle effect. If you are in a listen mode for someone and what you hear requires an action on your part, pay attention to your gut instincts and decide upon an action that will be appropriate. However, do not allow yourself to be triggered into a reaction. Think it through completely.

I am not advocating that you go nosing about in others' lives, but when it comes to your own, you must take an active role—in all of it. That includes the lives of those close to you. It can also include the lives of those who cross paths with you—especially if they are in need of assistance.

Many people are not willing to risk the possible karmic backlash from interfering in others' lives. But there will be times when you should interfere. If at such times you do nothing, rest assured you will encounter a karmic backlash for that just as quickly as you would had you performed the wrong action.

There is always the chance that the divine is using you as an instrument to move things along according to a higher plan. The anger manifests for a reason. You must allow yourself to see the possibility of a higher function before choosing a passive or aggressive role. There is always the chance you may regret an action you take, but it is far more common to regret an action you did not take.

Today, many wish to simply mind their own business and don't see that we are part of one whole. As magical practitioners, many things are our business that we have been ignoring. A particularly important phrase, coined in the sixties by Eldridge Cleaver is, "If you are not part of the solution, you are part of the problem." If you allow a problem to exist without making an effort to transform or defeat it, you are still a part of it, simply because you have the knowledge of its existence. As everything travels full circle, what do you think will come to you?

We are responsible for the world around us. If our world is not shaped to uphold our ideas, we can and should work to change that. The desire for positive change is the foundation of the principles of Anger Magic. It is our world; it is up to us to control it. Passive behavior may be the cornerstone of your ethics, but Angry Magicians (Anger Magic practitioners) need to take an aggressive stance.

An example of an aggressive stance would be that taken by a

lady in the discount store near me a few days ago. She ran into the store, upset and looking for a phone. She had witnessed a young mother lose her temper and slap her child's face several times. Immediately she wrote down the mother's license number and ran inside to call the police. We do not know all of what happened, but we do know the mother will think twice before hurting her child again. I say bravo to this woman. I commend her for taking an active role in a harmful situation. Had she ignored it, and the mother made a habit of it, the pain of that child—who she could have helped—would have had a full-circle effect back to her and possibly future generations of the child's family—which may have resulted in a continual cycle of pain with far-reaching consequences.

Anger Magic encourages intervention in negative cycles. We work to change them into something positive and to use the anger involved for destruction of the things that are negative and harm us.

You may wonder how I know that by making that phone call to the police, that woman was not interfering in the little girl's and the mother's soul journey through this life. Well, she was interfering, as I believe she was supposed to. People get so caught up in "interfering in another's journey" they forget the most basic of human behaviors. In this case, protect your young. Worrying so much about interfering—that you opt to do nothing—is an excuse to not face things that may indeed be hard to deal with. This stunts the growth of all the souls involved. Passivity can quickly become nightmarish. Calling the police is an example of the basic principles of Anger Magic. It could have been a mistake, but the woman took the chance and acted out of care and concern for the child. She looked at all of the available options and chose the one that held the most promise for a positive outcome for all.

There are lines that you don't cross as far as interfering in the lives of others, but when physical danger is present, do you want to risk inaction?

The state of our Earth displays the results of inaction. For example, it is much easier to let someone else deal with the population's garbage. As a result of our own inaction, we now live on a planet covered in trash that will not dissolve. Toxic chemicals are pouring into our water systems, and our forests and jungles are rapidly disappearing. If we continue on the passive path, the planet will be uninhabitable for humans before too long. We are destroying the future for the human race. This makes many of us justifiably angry. And one way to effect a change is to use Anger Magic.

Anger Magic is hard; it forces you to face things and try to change them. The goal is to re-create our world using an energy force that was once seen as dangerous. It is to use a power gifted to us from the divine, the gift of emotion. The true purpose anger serves is to destroy the negative influences in our lives. In our primitive human minds, we often get confused and use it to destroy the positive influences around us instead. We frequently lose sight of the full circle effect. Anger comes to us individually, so we tend to use it for individual purposes, which is fine. But we often forget to look at the whole. Anger serves many other purposes besides just destruction, all of which are healing or protective in nature.

It can be hard watching those we love struggle through growth issues and the pain that arises due to some of them. We cannot put ourselves on the line over normal issues. To do so diminishes our rights and power when it comes to tackling the bigger things. Divorce, losing a loved one, arguments, all are part of a normal growth system. You have to follow your heart and trust yourself to decide when something crosses the line into abuse. Abuse and violence are not part of a normal growth system. When we encounter them, we have both a right and a responsibility to act. Anger Magic is about action—how can you expect to harness an emotion and put it to work for you in a positive manner, if you are not willing to take a bit of control on the behalf of others too?

Angry actions require evolved personal ethics. No situation is ever exactly the same as another, and each must be evaluated and acted upon individually. Anger Magic requires the heart of a warrior; there will be times you will have to battle it out with negative influences.

It is easier to begin the battle within and work to destroy the negative influences surrounding your life before tackling the bigger issues that concern us all.

Before you can become a warrior and work on global issues, you must defeat your personal demons and you must do so alone. The heart and mind of a warrior must be pure in intent and clear of focus. If you have a problem with addiction, you must deal with it. If you have emotional baggage you are carrying around from childhood, you must face it. You do not have to rid yourself of all of that baggage; part of it has shaped you into who you are—but you do have to face it and know it. If the baggage contributes to seeing yourself in a negative light, however, you may want to be rid of it.

Some choices you face in Anger Magic will be clear and easy to read; you will immediately know what is right. Others will be muddied by emotion. Guilt and doubt may also come into play heavily in Anger Magic. Flexibility is key when dealing with a subject that touches upon you personally.

An example would be the young lady I know who was teased mercilessly throughout her childhood. She was poor, and children can be very cruel. They had put bars of soap in her locker, implying that because she was poor, she must stink as well. She suffered years of emotional trauma and low self-esteem because of the behavior of those kids. She is now a very successful banker. When it comes to dealing with teasing, however, her personal experience comes into play.

What some would consider part of a normal growth system, she sees as heinous. Teasing is unacceptable to her and goes against her personal ethics. The advantage this gives her is she knows where her line is drawn on this issue. The disadvantage is impartiality. It is almost impossible for her to be objective when faced with a teasing dilemma, due to her past trauma.

How she deals with this in her personal life is up to her. She may banish it, but by doing so will quite possibly no longer feel empathy to those undergoing what she endured as a child. She may choose to use it as a guardian for others experiencing the same sort of thing. Whatever she decides, if she follows the principles of Anger Magic, she will make use of the energy only after determining the most positive outcome.

5. Denying Yourself an Outlet

Some people are afraid of their anger. They remain passive and hope that time will heal all wounds. All too often it doesn't, it only dilutes the pain they cause. Once the emotion is diluted, you can no longer call them out with the original force, and yet you still may hurt just as much.

Anger exists in your heart, your mind, your soul, your body, and your vibrations. Ignoring it is not escaping it. Your options are use it or be used by it.

Denial of one's anger can manifest in a multitude of physical ways. Frustration can build up and bring about tension headaches, stomach and digestive disorders, nerve problems, high blood pressure, sexual dysfunction, jaw problems, back and neck troubles, and unbalanced emotions—and that's just to name a few!

Holding your anger inside the body can cause damage. Anger is simply not meant for the body. For the soul, it is a healing force, but when held in the flesh it will eat away at your health. It is wiser to channel it out and store it for later use. There is no need to waste such a potent energy.

From the point of view of a magical practitioner, holding in anger can be dangerous for other reasons. Magic manipulates energy by guiding it to areas where you will something to change. In order to manipulate energy you must be able to control it. Otherwise, you will have nothing to work with. You must be able to conjure and banish anger, and if you deny that it is even there you certainly can't use it.

Anger is useful—it teaches protection and value of the self. If you can allow yourself to be angry with others for wronging you,

you are validating yourself as a useful, needed part of the world. You have every right to your anger and every reason to use it to your advantage.

I have a dear friend who is facing a great loss. Her husband is terminally ill with stomach cancer. Because of the pain involved, he can be quite irritable. When the major painkillers he is taking dull his pain, they certainly dull his restraint. He often lashes out at her, verbally. On the rare occasion that she does fight back, she spends days in agony and regret over the things she said in retaliation. She is not allowing her emotions a form of healthy expression; rather she is denying them until they break out of their own accord. Because of this, she suffers from massive insecurity and a low self-image. She sees herself as one who could kick someone when they are down; when the truth is she is anything but that.

She allows him to take his anger out on her with the thought in mind of "being there" for him. Martyring yourself is not a positive action. It sets you up to see yourself as a victim. Not once has she realized that as she does so, she is soaking up his anger into her and not allowing it—or her own anger, for that matter—a healthy release. Therefore, it builds and builds, until it erupts like a volcano. She will not admit, even to herself, that she *is* angry. She sees anger in this case as a form of selfishness on her part. How dare she be angry with her husband when he is dying? She feels she should be sympathetic, or any of a dozen other emotions that she was raised to see as more appropriate. She doesn't deem herself worthy to feel the anger because the tragedy is not happening to her directly, she is not the one dying. But it *is* happening to her, too, and she has yet to realize the healing effects of *properly* expressed anger. In addition, not allowing herself that expression is one of the reasons she feels unworthy.

If you take only one thing to heart while reading this book, please make it this: You are always entitled to your emotion, whatever it may be. It is always appropriate to feel it, or your higher self would not have sent it to you. An emotion is not a decision.

There are no wrong emotions. Once you accept ownership of your emotion and entitlement to it, control comes easier.

We are conditioned as we grow up that it is not nice to act out of anger; we are often expected to learn how to control anger on our own. Rarely does a parent give a child the tools needed to work with anger. More often children are given a distorted view of the emotion and taught to think of it as wrong or bad.

You can see this on any playground. For example, a group of children are at play and one becomes angry and hits another child. The angry child is often scolded and told, "Nice young men or ladies don't hit others." But no one ever tells the child what actions are acceptable or what he can do with his anger that will benefit him. So he begins the process of repressing, and as an adult he may have problems with denial. He will relate anger to the scolding because of that earlier experience. Hence, anger is to be avoided in his mind and is bad.

Denial often has a snowball effect: What may begin as unexpressed anger relating to one area of your life will frequently overlap into other areas. By blocking the flow of one emotion, we effectively block them all and may begin to deny other things that are right in front of us. This process may begin as something as simple as becoming forgetful to pay the bills on time, or to take care of our bodies. It can quickly escalate into not seeing true danger. Anger offers us clarity only if we allow it to flow and give it a correct path to flow on.

I know a woman who, at the age of fifty-three, was unhappy in her home life. She was widowed, disabled, and living with her grown daughter and her daughter's family. When asked what she wanted to do about her current living situation, her response was, "How do I know what I want to do?" That sort of reply is the perfect example of a snowball effect. She had repressed her emotions to the point of not knowing her own mind. Even making the simplest decision was beyond her. Because of that, she tried to get the world around her to do her thinking for her; she had no trust in herself. In time, her lack of decision turned to just being lazy, from there it went to apathy. She victimized herself, and she did it by choice. She also burdened her daughter. By having to tend to all of the basic functions of adult thinking for her mother, the daughter lost sight of her own goals. She ended up feeling resentment and anger at her mother. This whole ongoing cycle stemmed from denial of anger.

This sort of behavior is unacceptable to an Anger Magician, who understands that everything we do travels full circle and that we cannot risk a backlash of inaction. At the same time we must be careful which action we choose to take, because for every action there is an equal and opposite reaction, for which we must be prepared.

Denial of anger for a magical practitioner can come into play in ritual settings or spell work. It can get in the way of meditation. It can become a barrier to your magic. In order to be adept at Anger Magic you must use it. The training can be long and hard, but it is worth it.

Not everyone will make use of the energy in the same manner, and as anger is an individual emotion, it is up to your sole discretion where you choose to make use of it. There are recommendations throughout this book, but in the long run it is you who must choose. All too often, the hardest part of Anger Magic is the free-thinking ethical system it requires.

Denying yourself the freedom to feel and express your anger in a healthy manner can cause you to explode or possibly implode. When we explode, we may hurt others with word or deed. We add to our karmic responsibility each time we do this. When we implode, we do damage to ourselves—mentally, physically, and emotionally.

Once anger is expressed properly, we find true mental clarity. If we maintain a clear focus we can use it productively.

Anger is an instinctual guide to the rights and wrongs of this life, and it is individual. We all walk the path a bit differently, but we can all benefit from self-control.

Denial of anger can affect the aura and chakra balance. When an aura is out of balance, it is more easily seen by lower astral entities. It may be seen as vulnerable. Lower astral entities feed from the energy of human beings; a strong protective aura keeps them away. If these entities see a muddled aura, they may attempt to attach. This can result in feelings of listlessness, chronic fatigue, headaches, and frequent bouts with depression, among other symptoms.

As magical practitioners, we are more open to universal vibrations than are other people. Having angry energy streams running wild through the universe is a great danger to others and us. Not taking ownership and control of our emotions causes this. By ignoring it, we are allowing others to be attacked by the free-flowing angry energy. Worse yet, not taking ownership for our own temper tantrums or anger bursts can include the fact that some of those wild energy streams bouncing around are ours. We will receive karmic payback for each person they touch.

Once the emotion has crossed the planes into our perception, it begins to take on "coloring." From that point, the vibrations will have a positive or negative feel. Once your emotion has been colored, it is irresponsible to disown or deny it.

In a case where you feel you may have contributed to wild anger vibrations, you may call your anger home. There is a ritual in chapter 27 with that intent. If you feel you are the recipient of someone else's wild anger, it is important to ground and release it or transform it and put it to good use.

There is a sad ending to this chapter. Over the course of writing this book, the husband of the friend mentioned in the cancer story earlier passed on. As she is facing her grief, she is currently blaming herself for feeling anger. She finally realized it was anger, but only after he had passed. She is trying to convince herself that his death is a punishment for her. She has yet to see that the anger was there to instill her with strength so that she could continue to care for him. He was going to die no matter what emotion she felt.

This is a classic example of a polluted pattern of emotion. His death was not "about" her, yet she is taking it upon herself by attempting to blame herself. Grief twists the mind. The death was not hers, but the grief certainly is. She does not realize that grieving is enough to cause others to sympathize with her, so she subconsciously tries to assume responsibility for the death as well. She has not reached the point of feeling worthy of her anger, and she continues to search for a way to punish herself. She is hoping the sympathy of others will be enough to pull her through her grief. However, feeling anger is a necessary step in the completion of the grieving process. In order for her to heal and reach a point of acceptance in regard to her loss, she first must allow herself to feel angry.

6. Proper Uses

The principles of Anger Magic are simple in instruction and can be complex on application. They assert:

1. Anger is a neutral form of energy; it is the human experience that allows it to take on a positive or negative quality.

2. All things are active. Inaction and reaction are actions in and of themselves.

3. All actions complete a full circle.

4. No two situations are ever exactly alike. Because of this, responses must be freethinking and flexible.

5. Practitioners have a responsibility to use anger in a positive manner by working to cancel out negative cycles.

6. Practitioners seek and accept control over emotions.

7. Anger is individual in perception.

8. Anger is of the divine, as such, it is pure.

9. Emotion exists as both an absolute and a relative influence and can be both at the same time.

10. Emotion can be both finite and infinite.

Let's go back to that child on the playground from the previous chapter. When he hit the other child, he did so because it was his instinct. It was a way for him to correct the wrongs in his perception of the world around him. It was an automatic "destroy feature," if you will. Without the knowledge of what constitutes a punitive action compared to a corrective action how can the child ever hope to master such a complex emotional process as dealing with anger positively, on an adult level?

Because the human race does not recognize anger as the positive power that it is, we have yet to develop the correct tools to allow us to deal with it in our most productive manner. We condition ourselves, and future generations, to avoid it entirely if possible. We have programs touting anger management to help us gain control, but they teach no real understanding of anger. Without understanding the basic premise of anger, those same programs reiterate the image of anger as "bad," with all its attendant negative stigma.

Mankind has a history of demonizing things it cannot understand or process in a simple way. Because anger is so misunderstood, it has gained a warped image and is viewed as incorrect. The fact is it is impossible for anger to be incorrect. It is eternal and infinite. It is of the divine and it is a pure energy. It is a vital tool for our survival and it exists on many planes and levels.

Emotions are at times so misunderstood that the human mind warps the experience of them into a perversion of their true purpose. Such is the case with anger. Anger holds purity until it reaches the human level. Once received into our brain, a process of dealing with it should proceed. How we process and deal with it is individual. If we deal with it in a correct and positive manner the purity will remain. If we twist it into what we want it to be, we have polluted it. Allowing ourselves to view anger in a negative light gives us a license to use it in a selfish way. Refusal to see it as a positive energy gives us an opportunity to continue to abuse the gift of anger. People can be selfish; they do not want to give up a view that suits them. By propagating the view of anger as a negative thing, they are free to continue their irrational and irresponsible behavior.

Not recognizing that anger is pure and of the divine, we often use it as an excuse for unimaginable cruelty. Torture, for example, which has no place in Anger Magic, is born of the human experience and resulting confusion of dealing with anger. Torture is a perversion of the pure form anger carries. It is the invention of a human mind and requires a cold-blooded outlook in order to perform it. Anger is hot and full of passion. It is not methodical in the least.

Often the torturers must reach such a state of detachment to their own actions that they may experience a soul displacement. They create a twin of themselves in their mind who is the person committing all of the horrible deeds. By so doing, they do not have to attribute the actions to themselves. This form of denial borders on self-hypnosis, but it carries much deeper consequences. It is from this displacement that the döppelganger and other such myths are born.

In effect, soul displacement is the splitting of a single soul. It can happen for many reasons other than anger, such as intense pain. Part of the soul fragments off into the creation of the doppelgänger. It can take many lifetimes to repair a split soul and call the pieces together as one again. Often a soul can split more than once, thereby increasing the time needed to come together as whole by several lifetimes. A displaced soul—or soul fragment—has no consciousness; only the original soul may retain full thought. The displaced part of the soul simply exists out of the selfish need of humans to compartmentalize their actions or reactions as acceptable.

The doppelgänger exists on Malkuth, the Earthbound plane whereas it could not exist in that form if it were an actual whole soul in and of itself. It is only a fragment. For that matter, ghosts could be attributed to soul displacement.

The important thing to note about soul fragments is the property of them. If they were created as a tool to help the original soul achieve a dishonorable purpose, such as torture, the quality of cruelty instilled in them will remain on Malkuth for future generations to deal with, even if the original soul has passed. The fragments remain on Malkuth until reunited with the original soul. Only then can the soul pass to the next level.

Learning to view your anger as a gift can be an eye-opening

experience. Mankind struggles with this needlessly. It is not the anger that creates a displaced soul or fragment; it is how we choose to relate to it. Soul fragments can be born from choice.

Anger is necessary to the soul as a force of change. It pushes the soul along its path, helping it to grow and shape it into what it is working to become. We hear the term "raging river," which is defined as a river moving quickly and forcefully. It is called *raging* because anger is seen as action, and rage is anger. Simply put, anger is an energy *force*. It is the force of anger that can allow for the creation of soul fragments, but only through our decisions.

At some point in our lives, we all deal with things that are so painful that it takes the force of anger to move beyond them. Our anger heals us by pushing us forward and making way for new beginnings, even when we are too hurt to do so on our own.

We fear what we perceive as being beyond our control and yet, we allow its existence outside of our control. Influences that exist within our realm of the emotional can be (and should be) under our absolute rule. As I have said, anywhere we allow our emotions to go should be consciously determined.

Because anger is attributed as a force, it is common for us to feel pressured as a direct result of coming into contact with it. The pressure may be immense, but because the anger belongs to you, it cannot burst through unless you allow it to do so.

It is when anger is perverted in the mind into a punitive force that the natural balance it holds begins to tip. The human race has a bloody history when it comes to punitive measures. From the Roman gladiator days to the Spanish Inquisition to death row today, punitive measures have deluded the human mind into forgetting that we are part of one whole. Indulgence in such perversions for reasons of punishment has no place in Anger Magic.

When dealing with punitive actions all too often equality ceases to be regarded as the eternal truth that it is. When equality is overlooked, it is from a perversion of the emotion, it is not of the divine. All beings have as equal value, no more and no less than any other being. All actions do not.

Religious and legal systems the world over still bear the marks of a society struggling to purify itself from natural influences, such as anger, which it has deemed as wrong or sinful. Barbaric practices born of misunderstanding emotional purpose continue to take place today. Female genital mutilation, executions for the smallest wrong, tortures, amputations, and the list just goes on and on. Brutality such as this is a human invention. It is not a property of anger and it is not from the divine.

Throughout your lifetime there will be people who will hurt you deeply. It is normal and natural to be angry with them. You may even wish to destroy them for hurting you. Realize, however, that a destructive response comes from the human mind. Anger Magic asserts taking an active role and doing so in a positive manner. We use the pure form of anger to shape the world into a more harmonious place. When faced with hurt, be it from a friend, loved one, or self, Anger Magic asserts that we use that hurt as an opportunity to improve our own circumstances and those of society.

Although punitive actions have no place in Anger Magic, justice certainly does. When we work for justice, we are not attempting to punish the person from a selfish need to be "right." We are calling for balance. If the divine decides on a punitive action, it does not mirror back to us in a full circle. The justice will, but not the punitive measure. What this means is, if calling for justice the full circle will complete with us. We may have to face a justice measure of our own from the divine. The action taken by the divine, however, punitive or otherwise, will not complete full circle to us, as the action was not ours.

Combating negative cycles also holds a place in Anger Magic. Working magically and mundanely to accomplish destruction of negativity is an important aspect of Anger Magic. In order to reshape our world we must get involved in it. Positive actions travel full circle too. In order to achieve blessings we must first earn them.

Because perception of anger is individual, we will all choose different things to work for. I may choose to work for improving ecology awareness or possibly my personal life and you may choose to work for the rights of children. As long as you are putting your anger to good use and improving the world around you, you are following the principles of Anger Magic.

Practitioners are often confused about how it is possible to destroy negativity as they see destruction in an equally negative light. Like anger, destruction is colored by the events surrounding it. If used for a positive intent, destruction holds nothing negative within it. If you are seeking to destroy an addiction to a drug that is doing grave harm to your body, for instance, destruction becomes a positive.

Nature eternally reflects a cycle of creation and destruction. There is nothing inherently negative about death or destruction, only in our perception of them. In order for the new to emerge, the old must give way. In order for a harmful cycle to cease, a positive one must begin. It is very possible to achieve destruction of negativity through creation. In other words, instilling the situation with enough positive influence can destroy the negative on its own, through the creation of a new and positive cycle. Seen in this way, creation *is* destruction.

7. Embracing Anger

I f you cannot hex, you cannot heal. There are myriad reasons to embrace your anger. It is only when used in an immature manner that anger can be dangerous. There are many reasons that anger is instilled within us, and one is for the purpose of self-defense.

A young woman I know got married at a very early age and proceeded to have children right away. The husband abused her physically and verbally. The time finally came when she could leave him, but he kept the children and restricted her time with them, claiming she was unstable. Weighed down and beaten, she did not fight his claim. He then went on to remarry and continued to verbally abuse her and allowed—and even encouraged—his new wife to do the same. This continued for years. Almost twenty years to the day of the original wedding, the woman finally got mad and began to fight back. She immediately had custody trans-ferred to her of the only daughter of the union, and respected the decision of the two sons to stay where they were because of their age. Overnight this woman gained control of her panic attacks—which had paralyzed her for years—and her life.

What was her final breaking point? The husband had the nerve to berate her relationship with her son and complained about her buying her son such a nice graduation gift, because he could not afford to do the same. That was like a bucket of icy cold water poured on her. It awakened her to the fact that nothing she could ever say or do would be suitable to him. Instead of rolling over and playing dead as she normally did, for the first time she recognized she was a victim. She knew that she was not the person he tried to make her out to be. She decided not to be his victim anymore.

When she made this decision, she did so as an action—not a reaction. She utilized her anger as a positive energy and brought about good changes to her life. Finding the courage to admit her anger gave her confidence and self-respect. Something she had been sorely lacking.

An odd side note about it is that as soon as she stood up for herself and would no longer fill the position of scapegoat for him, his marriage began to crumble. Her life fell into perfect alignment, his fell apart.

Sometimes anger may simmer beneath the surface and await the perfect moment to show itself. This is okay. A good stew must simmer a bit before it is ready to eat; all the spices and ingredients eventually come together in perfect harmony. How long it takes the stew is dependent on the base. My point is, don't rush it. The woman in the example took twenty years and it all ended up perfect.

I am by no means saying that you should bottle your anger up for twenty years, only that you do not allow for temper tantrums to erupt. Tantrums will only place you on the same level as your attacker. Venting anger in that manner will leave you very little power to draw from if and when the time comes for you to put your foot down about something.

You may purge your anger regularly if you desire, or you may transfer it to a storage facility until you can put it to better use.

Anger has an unfairly bad reputation. No one wants to be angry, but everyone wants to fall in love. But love can be truly dangerous, and when it goes wrong (as it so often does) the wounds may take a lifetime to heal. If you do manage to recover from a disastrous love relationship, you still may carry scars eternally. Many times, anger is a natural part of healing oneself from the pain of love gone wrong. It is the anger that heals you and moves you forward.

Am I telling you not to fall in love? Of course not! I am saying there is both a shadow side and a bright side to every emotion. In emotions, like ethics, nothing is ever purely black or white. You must know the emotion well enough to comprehend the opposite side of it—in order to use it in a positive manner.

Anger gives us confidence and strength. When used correctly, it boosts our self-esteem and balances the imbalances we may perceive in our world. It allows us to protect the things we love and to destroy the things that are harmful.

When it comes to magical work, the intensity of anger makes it perfect for use. Clarity is most often found in anger. Emotions are known to confuse, but in the case of anger, there is usually a stronger chance of focusing your will, thus achieving the desired goal.

We tend to equate anger and rage with destruction. However, anger is only energy. It is a careless response that causes unwanted destruction. If destruction is the goal of a well-thought-out plan for anger, you can destroy things that are harmful to you and improve your life.

It may help if you try to see your anger as a power surge, for that is what it truly is. Like a gift from the Goddess, it can be considered a direct order to you from your higher self. Anger, along with all of our other emotions, is a reminder that while we are in a human incarnation—we are of the divine. Anger is an instinct that exists for our survival in this life. It is your natural shield, and ignoring it may leave you defenseless. Wasting it—via tantrums and therefore gifting it to others—may leave you defenseless.

Anger can also be protective—not only self-protective, but protective, too, of those whom you love.

A woman I know used her anger as an inspiration. Raised in an abusive home, she got a job at the age of fourteen and began providing for herself. When she turned seventeen, she needed glasses and it fell to her to pay for the eye exam and buy them, or to do without. She continued working and bought them herself. Her father—in one of his rages—hit her on the head and broke her new glasses. Furious, she told him he would pay to have them replaced. She trembled and expected to be hit again. The father was in a state of shock. He was caught off guard by his daughter speaking to him in such a way, and he simply left the room. She felt the confidence and empowerment that using anger in a positive manner can bring. Soon afterward, she moved out and began life on her own terms. She had used her anger to overcome a childhood fear and was now ready to accept womanhood.

As many abused children unfortunately do, this woman married an abusive man. The marriage was rocky and she packed her bags and left him many times during the twelve years they were together. One day, she had enough and once again used her anger positively. She locked him out and calmly told him she would get the police involved if he did not go. He left; she was inspired again and went to college.

The above examples are important because they demonstrate the healing nature of anger. In both cases, the young woman was able to move forward, due to a healthy release of anger in everyday life.

When going through a particularly nasty time in life, we can be irrational and our anger is most often directed to those we love most. This sort of anger is usually not true anger at all; rather it is made up of frustration and feelings of helplessness. The anger we perceive it as is actually insecurity and hurt. We wear an angry mask to protect ourselves from further harm, hoping it will keep others away. While healing from the situation, we often find our true anger.

For instance, someone I know told me a story from their teen years. At the age of seventeen, she went through a tragic experience. She had felt pushed by her parents and abandoned by her boyfriend. Hurt, she did not speak to her boyfriend for six months. She wore a mask of anger and it all but shouted for others not to come near. But her behavior gave her the space she needed to heal, and at the end of her six months' retreat, she called her boyfriend. They are the best of friends today. Even when it's only a mask for other feelings, anger can be a powerful protector.

As I have said, anger magically propels things forward at a "furious" pace. There is nothing in the universe it can't reach.

8. Critical Points of Working with Anger in Magic

We walk a fine line when dealing with anger in magic. We will individually address each issue you may encounter while working with Anger Magic.

Some of the problems you may run into are heat instability, volatility, problems in the transformation process, self-blame, excessive buildup, dealing with the magical properties of anger, feelings of pressure or stress, the high speed of anger, and the systematic chain of emotions anger generates. All of these problems have solutions.

Let's tackle heat instability first. The magical property of raw anger is hot. When working with it your body heat may be affected. One of two things may happen. You will either feel your body temperature go up or down. If it goes down, then the transformation process is in place and working. Mother Nature forces this balance as a signal to let us know the energy around us is changing. If it rises, we are still in the building stage and need to keep going until it begins to drop. An important note here is if your body temperature rises then drops back to normal range, it is still considered a drop and means the change is occurring. Furthermore, if the building stage is just too overwhelming and you begin to become overheated, or have a hard time catching your breath, channel some of the energy into a storage facility immediately. Do not risk your health.

If your body temperature drops dramatically at the very beginning, stop. You are in need of purging. Remember the term "cold-blooded," and do not go forward until heat has been built up.

You could also run into electrical problems in the area. Anger can blow lightbulbs and short out electrical switches. This may freak you out a bit at first—if you experience it at all—but it is common and should be expected.

A little quirk concerning the magical properties of anger is the possibility of small explosions. If you have carbonated beverages nearby, dispose of them prior to engaging anger in magical work. The reaction they have with anger can be distracting and a bit messy. Also due to this, candles may have a tendency to pop and the flame may grow quite large. This, too, is normal—so try not to be overly worried about it.

Another magical property of anger is sourness. It may be a taste in the mouth or a smell in the air. Its presence may even sting your eyes. To combat these effects, open a window and let in some fresh air, burn incense, and be sure to drink plenty of water. (If you have an expensive cream liquor or the like nearby, you may want to put it away to minimize the risk of souring.)

Because anger has the property of sourness, it is best to perform Anger Magic on an empty stomach. One particularly nasty side effect of working Anger Magic after a meal is the potential of vomiting. A ritual fast beforehand—even only if for a few hours—is a good idea to counteract the potential of "sour stomach."

Another potential problem is the high speed of anger. Anger moves in an instant. It's hard to get a grip on it in everyday life and can certainly be tricky when using it for magic. The best solution for this is to cast a sacred circle, to contain the energy until you are ready to let it go.

The cure for excessive speed is time. Hold the energy until such a time that you are positive it is ready to be released. Anger moves on its own speed once released. Do not be in a rush to let it go. A common trick we play on ourselves is allowing ourselves to be rushed. We must combat this by carefully taking our time, no matter how much we need.

On the astral plane, where emotions exist as form, time works in a different manner than it does on Malkuth (the Earth-bound plane). A perceived need to rush is common whenever the plane is crossed because time is not equal in both places. Take the current world currency for example; one dollar in American money may equal seventy cents in another country. It is much the same kind of exchange when emotions cross over astral boundaries. You may only have room for twenty-five cents and find yourself faced with hundreds of coins. Because we are working on this plane, we must allow ourselves the time we need to complete the task.

Because of anger's unequal transfer, compounded by the fact that anger is an energy *force*, the feeling of needing to rush can be profound. Being unaware of this effect can cause some people to erupt into tantrums and rages.

Opposite to this is the possible lag factor, the kind of anger that sneaks up on you at a later time. People who suffer from post-traumatic stress disorder (PTSD) regularly experience this kind of anger. You still must take your time, as much as you need. Sometimes when trauma occurs we experience shock; we may freeze and find ourselves witnesses to our own victimization—as if you are lifted from your body and are no longer a participant in the event. This is a natural response. It is when the anger comes along later that people get confused. What they often fail to realize is the purpose for the lag time. Once anger is present, it is there to force a healing. The lag time comes from our higher self, to give us adequate time to fully ingest the data of what happened. The anger may not appear until we feel safe again, because until then, we cannot heal.

You may also run into problems with excessive buildup of anger. It can block your growth if you do not keep the channels clear. Absorbing crystals or charcoal chunks may be placed on your chakra points to help keep the channels clear and to maintain a more balanced energy flow.

To store your anger, find a suitable facility. It can be a statue, fetish, or crystal. It can be a covered container of dirt or salt for instant neutralization. It can be anything you like, but it is important to make sure no one else can get to it. Better to keep it under lock and key and keep the energy pure and unique to you. A storage chest full of anger is not the type of thing you want others to stumble upon.

To channel the feeling into the facility you can use touch and hold the object in your right hand sending the vibrations through your arms, hands, and fingers into the object. You can use your mind and project the vibrations into the object through your eyes or your third eye, the energy vortex that exists in the center of your forehead. You can send the vibration through a tool (such as a wand) and into the object, or you can use incense and "smoke" it in. You can even use your breath and blow it in, or simply use your voice and command it to go there.

If you do not want to store your excess anger for later use, consider purging it altogether. For this purpose, I recommend using Earth and Water. Anger has the properties of Air and Fire; to neutralize it we need to balance it out. Salt is especially good for this and a saltwater purge is the best around: You may swim in the ocean as a purge, or add bath salts to your bath. Or you can mix salty water in a bowl and send the vibrations into it. You may even wish to double purge and send the anger to a pot of saltwater that you can then boil. Err on the side of caution and do the boiling outside, simply on the off chance that a bit of unresolved anger may waft through on the steam. This is extremely unlikely, but it is better to be sure that it can't happen at all.

Tears are a salty form of water and a wonderful purge that can truly make way for healing. Other than that, anything that will call the elements into balance will serve you well as a purge: like making a mud pie and pounding the anger in, for example. When you mix the mud back with the dirt on the property you took it from, it is proper to ask it be used for good but not absolutely necessary. Purging into a stream or creek is acceptable. Water instantly balances (cools) the anger, so there is no need to fear that you will harm fish or other wildlife. For those who live in the city, watching your anger swirl down the drain can be a profound purging experience.

You may be wondering how it is possible to feed a plant anger without a natural balance taking place and canceling it out. By placing the anger in the eggshell, we are protecting it. The candle wax has an absorbent quality; therefore, even if we powder the shell, the essence remains in the shell fragments.

It is normal to encounter problems of self-blame. A common emotion elicited by anger is doubt. You could start to wonder if you are doing the right thing, or think maybe it really is your fault. The best counterpoint for this problem is separation. Allow your anger—within the confines of your circle—to take on a separate identity. This can be dangerous, so every precaution must be taken when setting up the circle. Every possible barrier should be named—identified and stated. The sole purpose of the anger conjuration must be defined by you, verbally, to be only for viewing purposes, and to be completely powerless. It exists only for your examination. Allow it to take form in a circle within your circle and do not allow it to move. Keep in mind that you are harming no one with this action, as it is your emotion you are conjuring and you have every right to control it. This may remind you a bit of summoning spirits and in fact it is quite similar in practice. In actuality, it can be more like summoning a demon. You just cannot be sure of what you will uncover. Keep to heart with it, though, because it is not some other world being, it is a part of you.

The precautions are because you may uncover something forgotten and explosive in nature. While doing this, have a bucket of water in your circle, just in case. It is always better to be safe than sorry. When you are done, send the energy back or send it on. You may transform it and send it where needed, neutralize it or purge it. Your anger is there for your bidding.

If you have a hard time allowing your anger to exist outside of yourself, you could use a simulation to bring it out or a meditation to examine it from within. To simulate you need to recreate the magical properties. One particularly effective way is to burn sulfur. I do not recommend doing that inside. Sulfur has a very unpleasant odor and stings the eyes. It is hard to breathe around burning sulfur for many people.

About defining your barriers: energy flows. If there is a crack in a surface, energy will find it. It is up to you to see to it that does not happen. A universal rule is like attracts like and on a vibrational level that is certainly true. Knowing that rule is key to seeing which areas of your life could be affected from a spell using an anger generator. Anger in magic must be controlled completely and given no room to go wild. If you wish to use it to stop smoking, for example, you must not allow the energy to wander from that set course. You must seal up all cracks before beginning.

You should set up your barriers when you cast your circle. This can be done with a verbal command such as, "I will that the energy conjured in this rite be completely controlled by me. It may only go where directed and it specifically may not go to ———." Seek out the parallels to help determine which areas may need particular guarding. If you properly identify the problem areas, you can set up impenetrable barriers, thus reducing your risk of the anger mirroring back to you in a harmful fashion.

It is a good idea to ask the guardians to maintain the integrity of your circle with you. You can back it up with extra protection by doing something along the lines of driving iron stakes in the ground around the circle. You may do anything that you feel will help contain the energy.

Be aware that anger attracts every other emotion. The system it chooses to flow in varies, but often it is your release method that decides the order of emotions elicited. If you release it in a healthy manner, you will feel empowered and confident. If you release it in an unhealthy manner, you may feel afraid and doubtful. This is under your control, so there is no reason why Anger Magic cannot be used for positive works.

Anger has the ability to overwhelm the physical body, but not the mind or soul. What may be perceived to be losing control is a common occurrence when an emotion crosses over planes; it is hard for the physical body to take charge of it.

Your spirit resides on the astral plane with emotions, and in your body at the same time, through a link in the mind. The link is that of the "higher self" to your consciousness and it is found in your subconscious. The conscious is in the mind; the subconscious is in the whole. This is where the term "gut reaction" comes from.

Occultists sometimes use the term "silver cord" to speak of this link. It is not really important to your work here to find the seat of the soul (or origins of the link) but rather to acknowledge its existence. Once you understand that you are tied to the same plane as emotion through spirit, you can make use of this knowledge to bring about change. Finding your keys to balance the crossover will enable you to achieve harmony on *both* planes.

Problems in the transformation process are most often caused by the unbalanced crossing over of planes. Since emotions exist as form on the astral, they have weight. They exist only as invisible patterns of feeling on Malkuth and have no form or density that you can measure. There are two exceptions to this rule. The two emotions that have a weighted effect on the soul on Malkuth are sadness and anger. We hear frequently of people who feel they cannot control emotion and that is because they do not understand the connection between the realms.

Think of it like this: The emotional crossover is like a huge electrical fuse box. The higher self is a conduit. It sends the emotion needed from one plane to the spirit in need on the other. Sometimes a channel is blocked and it must send enough to re-open it. Sometimes you are caught unaware by this and receive a "surge." Learning which size circuit breaker you have, and installing the one you need will be the key to not blowing all of your fuses.

Before learning how to do this, you may have unknowingly flipped the circuit off or had it flipped by the surge. Learning to program your breakers to fit you, based on our past experiences, can allow for a smooth transition of energy, with no worry of blowing your fuses.

It is when the "flips" occurred that you might have experienced loss of control. In order to control the energy flow, you must install the correct circuit breakers. The emotion itself is the raw electricity.

To help you understand and perform the installation process, see the exercises in chapters 9, 10, and 11. Indeed, simply understanding the process of the crossover has most likely brought your mind to exactly where it needs to be and quite possibly installed the proper breaker for you. The mind is a miracle and the knowledge of need is usually instantly fulfilled on that level.

Transformers—like those that sit on electrical poles—serve a function in the magical fuse box of energy exchange also. Transformation should follow a stringlike pattern. Emotion → energy → idea. On the astral plane, it is emotion in form, we receive it as energy, and we put it to use by transforming that energy into an idea. Control is within the mind.

Outside of this, we can utilize insulators—which work as safety nets. Common insulators are comfort foods, certain aromatherapies, sexual release, bubble baths, hot tea, certain colors, comforting music, and ambiance. Our homes are usually filled with insulators that we may not recognize as such. If an object or action brings about a warm, comforting feeling, it can be used as an insulator. Even something as trivial as the coffee mug a friend gave you last Yule can be used for this purpose. You just have to open your eyes to your surroundings.

All electrical generators have a grounding wire, but in this case it is unique to the person. It may be a treasured pendant or ring. It could be a favored statue of your matron goddess. It could be the

Earth itself. Search to find yours. You may use traditional ground-ing methods as a substitute until you find the one you feel is per-fect for you.

A special note about hot flashes: Women in the premenopausal and menopausal stages of life experience power surges on a regu-lar basis. They are called "hot flashes," and they are really a signal from the divine. Their purpose is to remind you of the duality of your existence. You are at once experiencing an aging of body on Malkuth and an aging of soul on the astral. Too often, you may focus on one and forget the other. While being dismayed by your body's aging, you may lose sight of the fact that it is the soul's *goal* to age and grow.

Hot flashes signal that the higher self is moving closer to the body. It still stands between the worlds but is gravitating a bit closer.

Hot flashes are raw power from a woman's soul. Astral projec-tion—if employed during a hot flash—can be a profound experi-ence and one that nothing on Malkuth can equal. Pay very close attention to your thought patterns during hot flashes. Visions of the astral are common and you may be having them without real-izing it. Women experiencing hormonal fluctuations have a vast store of power open to them. If it is menopausal in origin, they usually have the wisdom and seasoning to balance their work with Anger Magic quite well.

Patterns: When working with anger the patterns are important. If seeking to build anger use a widdershin (counterclockwise) pat-tern. If wishing to dissolve anger use a Deosil (clockwise) pattern. These are not the patterns of casting your circle, only for the work that commences after you have done so. The circle should be cast using your usual method.

In chapter 7 we talked a bit about allowing your anger time to meld—as if in a stew. While that is a good analogy, it would be a bad practice. Anger has no business in the kitchen during food preparation. If you feel like working out your anger by kneading bread dough, for example, it is best that you do not allow anyone to eat the bread you have made for the purpose.

After using anger in magic, you must make it a practice to cleanse and ground. The cleansing is absolutely necessary—so do not let it slide. Cleanse yourself and the area you have worked in each time. Basil, black pepper, and salt sprinkled about the area work well to dispel any remaining negative energies and to restore calm at the same time.

II. Learning the Art of Control

Tactics and Self-Help

9. Exercises to Harness Angry Energy

nger is fleeting; it moves across planes in an instant. One method of learning to control anger—and tap into it for magical use—is to harness it. In effect, this will allow you to direct your anger as well as to "ride the wave." Some of you will learn how to control it internally, others will learn externally. The following exercises will encompass both methods.

Anger transfers across the planes, into our existence, via our higher self, and reaches us in our minds. It begins its journey on our plane in the left brain. Control does not normally happen until the energy transfers itself to our right brain—where it forms into an idea.

The left brain is home primarily to logical thoughts and does not process emotion well. Emotion in the left brain leads to re-action, so we need to enroll the right brain for understanding. The right brain deals best with feelings. By realizing our triggers, and listening to our bodies' response patterns, we can logically track anger down to a left-brain function. We can also seek to control it from the left brain before it ever changes from raw energy into the idea of feelings. If you do not succeed with left-brain control, don't worry: You can always control anger using a right-brain perspective. This is what I mean when I say some people learn internally (left brain), and others externally (right brain).

The learning method (internal or external) is not the important point for magical work, only for controlling experience. For actual magical work, the energy will be channeled out of the whole body and soul into a raw energy stream. It doesn't matter which side it comes from, only that it is all out.

You should follow a daily program of performing the following meditations to "install" your circuit breakers. I recommend doing the meditations every day, focusing on one meditation for four weeks at a time. It is imperative that you perform the meditations in order. Follow at least a thirty-day cycle; it is crucial to ensure full installation. Along these lines, I should note that only the function of the meditation changes as you progress. The journey stays similar throughout the series for comfort reasons.

If you wish to cast a circle or build a focus table for the following meditations, do so (more information on this can be found in chapter 14). Whatever makes you comfortable becomes the rule. Remember to take deep rhythmic breaths and relax your body.

Once you have completed the four-week cycles of each of the three meditations in this chapter, you may progress to the meditations in chapter 14. The exercises should be performed daily, at least one or two of them, until they become habitual. This usually takes at least thirty days per exercise.

Meditation Sequence

Meditation One: See yourself sitting on a patch of warm sunny grass in the middle of a beautiful field. The sun is warm and the air is fresh. Close your eyes and stretch out to enjoy the warmth of the sun. As your eyes close, it becomes dark but remains warm. Safe and comfortable, allow yourself to daydream a bit. You walk down a dimly lit path and come to a door. You look closely at the door, determining its size, color, and texture. You wonder what is on the other side of the door, and you reach out to touch it. You put your hand on the knob and turn it. As the door swings open, you see a large space. It is filled with data, all sorted logically and filed neatly. You realize that you have just opened the door to the left side of your brain. On a table in front of you sits a neatly printed list. You walk to it and pick it up. You read that it is a list of signals that your left brain sends to your right brain when it receives an emotion. You study the list carefully, noting crucial information. You place the list back on the table for future viewing and turn to leave. You close the door behind you. You begin walking back down the dimly lit path. You arrive at the warm patch of sunshine and open your eyes. You stretch out and enjoy the patch of sunny grass for a moment, contemplating all that you learned. You are back in your body. Right here and right now. Take out your journal and write the signals you remember in it, as well as any notes about your journey.

Meditation Two: Envision yourself sitting on a patch of warm sunny grass in the middle of a beautiful field. The sun is warm and the air is fresh. You close your eyes and stretch out to enjoy the warmth of the sun. As your eyes close, it becomes dark but remains warm. Safe and comfortable, you allow yourself to daydream a bit. You walk down a dimly lit path and come to a door. You look closely at the door, determining its size, color and texture. You reach out to touch it. Just before your fingers make contact, the door begins to change. As you watch, it transforms itself into a large gray metal box. You notice that the box has wires running to it and into the dark. You cannot see what it is connected to. You notice the box has a panel that opens it and you reach out and pull it open. You look inside and see circuit breakers neatly aligned, in two vertical rows. You look closely, determining which breakers have been flipped to the off position. You have to look hard to see the writing on the breakers, but it becomes clearer as you take your time to examine it. When you find a breaker that is tripped because it is too small to handle the circuit weight, you make a mental note to remember it. You touch each breaker to remember the feel of it and you prepare to leave. You begin walking back down the dimly lit path. You arrive at the warm patch of sunshine and open your eyes. You stretch out and enjoy the patch of sunny grass for a moment, contemplating all that you learned. You are back in your body. Right here and right now. Take out your journal and write in it about the breakers you changed, as well as any other notes about your journey.

Meditation Three: See yourself sitting on a patch of warm sunny grass in the middle of a beautiful field. The sun is warm and the air is fresh. You close your eyes and stretch out to enjoy the warmth of the sun. As your eyes close, it becomes dark but remains warm. Safe and comfortable, you allow yourself to daydream a bit. You walk down a dimly lit path and come to a door. You look closely at the door, determining its size, color, and texture. You reach out to touch it. Before your fingers make contact, the door begins to change. As you watch, it transforms itself into a large gray metal box. You notice that the box has wires running to it and into the dark. You cannot see what it is connected to. You notice the box has a panel that opens it and you reach out and pull it open. You look inside and see circuit breakers neatly aligned, in two vertical rows. You look closely, determining which breakers have been flipped to the off position. You have to look hard to see the writing on the breakers but it becomes clearer as you take your time and examine it. When you find a breaker that is tripped because it is too small to handle the circuit weight, you exchange it for one of the right size. Once all the circuit breakers are installed in the correct areas, you prepare to leave. You begin walking back down the dimly lit path. You arrive at the warm patch of sunshine and open your eyes. You stretch out and enjoy the patch of sunny grass for a moment, contemplating all that you learned. You are back in your body. Right here and right now. Take out your journal and write in it which breakers you changed, as well as any notes about your journey.

Exercises

I recommend performing the exercises each time you are in a situation involving anger—or facing the possibility of anger. You may also strengthen the process by writing or saying affirmations daily. It will help with some of the exercises to have a definite symbol—such as a black dot or a red solar cross—in mind to represent the anger.

The Red Mist Exercise that follows is a visualization. I recommend practicing this exercise in a sacred circle, for simple containment reasons. I also recommend doing it gradually. Start with small irritations and build your way up to rage situations. I do not recommend the Red Mist Exercise if you have a history of asthma or breathing problems.

Red Mist Exercise: Visualize your anger as a red mist. It slowly hovers toward you and you breathe it in. Allow it to collect in your lungs. Move it through your body—from anywhere it may linger—to your lungs. Blow it out. It is bright red and pulsating with energy. Breathe it back in and hold it for a few seconds.

Now take a balloon—you may color correspond with an intention, if you like—and blow the red, angry energy into the balloon. Blow hard and leave no breath in your body. You now have control of your anger in an external incarnation. You may substitute a bag or soap bubbles. The point is to release it from its internal position and to capture it externally.

Once you have the red breath visualization down and can see it clearly in your mind, begin to release your breath slowly. You may use a drinking straw or narrow tube to help you achieve this. Blowing up a balloon in a steady stream of air is no easy feat, but as we are internalizing our anger in our breath, we must be able to control it there. If you cannot blow up a balloon that way, substitute soap bubbles or just blow air through the straw. Make sure to hold the anger true to the visualization of red mist throughout.

The Lightning-Click Exercise: Visualize your anger as lightning striking the big metal fuse box. Each time it strikes, you hear a click. You open the door to the fuse box and see all the circuits intact and in the on position. The click is simply a signal, similar to a knock on a door, that heralds the arrival of energy.

Focusing on the lightning can help us to avoid acting on the anger at that moment. Refusing to see the energy as anything other than raw energy will add strength to the focus.

This exercise also helps relieve any doubts about our circuit breakers, as the lightning "tests" them with each strike. Learning the strike pattern can help us in harnessing. Often our strike patterns are repetitious.

The Maintenance Exercise: To maintain control we must keep continual watch on our circuit breakers. As an exercise, write a maintenance meditation in which you perform all the necessary tests and changes to the breaker box. It is best to follow the format you have already learned—from the meditation sequence—when dealing with the fuse box, as you want it to become routine behavior. The more you acquaint your mind with the procedure, the faster you will accomplish the desired function.

It is important to write a maintenance meditation yourself, because only you can identify any possible problems before they occur.

The Circle Exercise: In this exercise, we seek to harness our anger within the defined barrier of a circle. It should be done daily, optimally in the morning, and you will need a ring or a necklace as a circle remembrance, to wear for the day.

Put on your ring or necklace and say, "My anger is mine. I control it and keep it. As this ring/necklace forms an unbroken connection around my body so, too, do I remain connected to my anger. I do not give it away, but I will it to go where I wish." Repeat the affirmation ten times.

The Silver Lasso: The Silver Lasso Exercise is a visualization that combines seeing your anger in a tangible form and watching yourself harness it. Choose a symbol to represent your anger. Any symbol that makes you think of anger will do—even a red dot is fine. Visualize your anger as that symbol floating directly in front of you. As you watch, it begins to drift slowly away. You watch the anger move farther away from you. You decide to capture it. See the top of your head open as a silver lasso springs from your crown chakra. The lasso twirls in the air and whips itself toward the anger symbol. It closes tightly on the anger and begins to pull it home. When it returns to the crown chakra the top of the head closes and the anger is contained within, but held immobile by the silver cord.

Subliminal affirmations can be utilized in the background to further your control work a bit more. A good rule of thumb to follow is that anytime you are doing mind work, wisdom dictates that you adhere to a thirty-day plan. Self-hypnosis can also be tailored to fit into your program. If you don't have the fancy gadgets such as computer programs or sound boards needed to design subliminal affirmations, you can design them the old-fashioned way. Write the affirmation(s) on paper repeatedly. Say it out loud several times a day. As long as you remind yourself daily of the goal it will work in the same manner as would a subliminal tape recording.

10. Exercises to Recycle and Transform Energy

hese transformation exercises are based in nature. We will use the four elements to help us to transform anger into raw energy. The anger should have been previously built and transferred to a proper receptacle or should be present within you. These exercises assume the presence of anger.

You may be wondering how it is possible to "fight fire with fire" and call upon that element for use in anger transformation. Fire has a purifying ability, and when two separate and distinct fires meet one can easily burn the other out.

Earth

Nothing can do a more complete job of transforming energy than the Earth element. When you bring Earth element into an angry working, you bring balance—so you must keep it at a lower level than the anger or risk canceling out the energy completely.

Take your storage facility outdoors and sit under a nice tree with calm energies. Smell the rich fragrance, feel the bark, relax, and just get to know the tree. Place your storage facility upon a gray cloth at the bottom of the tree. Tell the tree what the facility holds and how you would like to use it. Wrap it in the cloth and bury it for three days. When you come to retrieve it three days later, make sure to bring a token for the tree as a thank you.

If a tree is not available to you, you can use a potted plant for the same purpose. You just need to adjust the timing factor. A small plant can take up to ten days to transform the energy.

The gray cloth is an important part of the transformation process. It provides a barrier to keep the energy contained at the same time that it allows the tree or plant to neutralize the energy by passing vibrations through it.

Granted, the previous exercise was more of a transformational method, but the more you practice with it, the quicker you will get the hang of knowing when the energy has been neutralized. You never know what little "tweaks" you may have to do to personalize an exercise. Since you are dealing with your own personal energy, tweaks can be expected and are considered a good thing.

Another Earth-oriented exercise calls for a visualization. See your anger as the Earth herself. See her surface begin to crack in a giant earthquake. She yawns wide and does so in a screaming fury. You throw an object into her center and wait. A few moments later, she spits it back to you as raw, pulsating energy, and then she closes herself back up. Taking your time with this method and visualizing it thoroughly leads to a well-transformed emotion. The results are very satisfying.

Anger relates to the crown chakra, which is why putting on a hat in times of anger and stress can be successful as a blocker. For this exercise, you will need a box of sand. Allow the anger to collect in your crown chakra. Bend over and visualize yourself opening the top of your head. Allow your anger to pour into the sand. Wait patiently until it is all out. Once the anger is released from the chakra and positioned in the sand, you can proceed with essential oils or herbs and scent the sand. I suggest scenting it with something you relate to as tranquil and peaceful, like lavender or rosemary. You may then take a miniature rake and a few stones and transform the sand into a Zen garden, raking it into a soothing pattern.

You may also wish to attempt attracting lightning to your sand. Lightning signifies change and is transforming in itself. Simply spread your sand around a lightning rod and wait for a storm. Cast a circle (not too close, obviously) to stay in place while you wait.

When and if lightning strikes the sand you will have a unique formation of fused sand or natural glass. You may choose to shape it into a vessel to hold your anger. It is important to note here that sand may be used over and over throughout the year and you can plan the lightning procedure to coincide with peak storm seasons, according to your geography. Sand is unique in that it will never fill up completely with emotion, but it can contain massive amounts.

Fire

When working with fire always follow basic safety precautions. The use of fire in transformation is simple. You may write the anger down and announce that by flame it becomes pure and then burn it. For example, if you are mad at your boss, write it down. Write the who, what, when, where, why and how. Leave nothing out. Charge an indigo candle with the task of transforming the energy. Light the candle, hold up your paper, and say, "By this flame the energy contained on this paper becomes pure. I may direct it where I wish." Decide the direction and state it aloud. Now burn the paper and blow away the ashes.

You may place a stone directly in the flame and transform the energy it contains that way, but I recommend doing this only out of doors. Some stones are explosive when placed in (or around) a fire. Magical crystals are usually safe to use, but riverbed or damp stones may explode due to their moisture content. You would need to channel all the anger into the stone or use a stone that has been a storage facility prior to this act.

Fire cleansing cannot erase your stone if that is the intent you set. For the purpose of this exercise, we will be transforming the energy into raw energy and so do not wish to erase it.

I suggest performing this exercise either using a cauldron or a small outdoor fire ring. Get the flames going strong and drop in your stone. Verbally affirm, "By the flames that cleanse, I ask that the energy contained in this stone be transformed back into raw energy. No longer is it angry, but it remains mine and will be put to good use." Allow the fire to burn out on its own. Once the stone is cool enough you may pluck it from the ashes. You can allow yourself comfort in knowing this method is foolproof. In chapter 11 you will find methods to release the energy.

Air

Energy transformation and air go hand in hand with visualization. Another method of utilizing air for transformation is use of the breath. You may also enlist the winds.

When working with air in Anger Magic you may do so with a storage facility or without. You can visualize the anger as a cloud, for example, and work to transform it from there.

Cast a circle, call your anger up through your chakras, one by one, and send it out through your right index finger. Watch it hover about, right in front of you. Look at it—hard. Concentrate on it and visualize it beginning to churn. As you watch, it grows stronger. Now concentrate on changing it. See it begin to turn into a white pulsating light of pure energy. (Do not rush this, it could be instant or it could take hours.) Reach out and touch it; you should feel a quick power surge. If your visualization alone is not enough to transform it, add air by virtue of breathing toward it or call the winds of change for aid.

The wind has a fury all of her own at times and can be a powerful force to add to your magic. You may use the power of a storm or conjure a visualized storm to accomplish the transformation. See a hurricane encompass the anger and "purify" it. You will need a symbolic representation of your anger in order to capture the lessons in this type of exercise, perhaps even something as simple as a black dot.

You may also take a piece of cord or rope and tie anger knots into it. Channel the anger into the cord and tie it into a tight knot, trapping the anger in place. You may smoke the rope or cord with smoke from burning sage to transform the anger back into raw energy. Later, simply untie the knots to release the energy.

Water

Running water is a natural cleansing agent. If your wish is to transform energy, you will do better using still water, unless, of course, you want to use it strictly for a visualization. Visualizing a tidal wave will transform the anger, but actually using a physical form of running water will erase the anger.

Seeing your anger in a flowing pattern, as we do water, can be a boon to mastering control as well as transformation. For this exercise, we will seek to pour our anger—as we would water—into a glass or similar container. After mastering this, you can freely pour the energy into a spell or wherever you decide to place it.

As disgusting as the thought may perhaps be, one way to try to look at anger is as a sort of acid reflux: Visualize your anger building in your throat. In a fluid manner, it builds and swells up to the back of your mouth. You may taste it; it will be sour. Open your mouth and see a red wave roll out and into the container in front of you. If this exercise makes you feel ill, stop it. If you are comfortable performing it, you may repeat it until it becomes a natural function.

Of course, you may also choose to visualize projecting the fluid from your third eye or crown chakra.

Baths are also a good way of purging excess anger. If you add a touch of lavender and a piece of rose quartz to the water, you will feel the angry energy begin to disperse almost immediately. A nice, long, relaxing soak in the tub can be very beneficial in many different ways.

II. Exercises to Release

t is imperative that we practice releasing excess anger on a regular basis. The more we practice the releasing exercises, the easier it is to control the flow of emotion. We can set it in our minds to allow the excess to flow directly through us, thus minimizing internal conflict.

Grounding Wire Exercise

There are two ways to approach this exercise. You can see the grounding wire as an extension from your feet into the Earth, or you can see it as an extension from your tailbone into the Earth. In both cases, it will act as an invisible link, a connection from ourselves to the Earth below us.

The function of the grounding wire is twofold. It allows for drainage of excess energy and it can draw needed energy from the Earth into our bodies. Simple control of the grounding wire allows us to purge routinely with very little thought about it, throughout the day.

For this exercise, we will be "blasting" the wire open. We will draw energy bundles into our bodies from the Earth, via the wire, allow the energy to build, and forcefully send it back. We are in effect blowing the tubes out, to eliminate any obstructions.

Stand with your feet hip distance apart and begin to draw energy up through your wire in a slow, relaxed manner. Continue until you feel you cannot contain any more. Hold it a few seconds, and then send it all back at once. Push it through the wire as though it were propelled forward by the force of an explosion. Do this five times. You may use this exercise any time you feel you need to, it helps to keep your grounding wire functioning in top form.

You may also wish to exercise your drawing ability, and pull energy up a few times each day. I encourage you to do this as it helps program the function into your mind, so that it becomes natural to you.

Sexual Release

You may find this exercise a bit out of the ordinary. However, it is one of the best ways to release energy from the body. I will attempt to be delicate.

The relation between anger and sex is natural. When your body is flushed with energy, it's normal for the energy to run a sexual course too. When combining Anger Magic with sexual release, you should make a personal decision whether you wish to invite another to share it with you. Be aware that there can be many problems if you do. You may induce karmic risk if you do not inform the other person of the angry energy that will be present, and there is also a high risk that you may become distracted from your intent and abandon it at a crucial moment. Using birth control is a necessity, not an option. Never, ever attempt sexual anger release without a sacred circle in place.

For the purposes of this exercise, you are far better off going it alone. Yes, I mean masturbation. Have a storage facility nearby, and at the moment of sexual release, channel all of that power into the object. You can place crystals nearby for this purpose.

Allowing your anger to reach the point of perverted thoughts is okay. You do not have to monitor your every thought—in fact, I recommend that you don't. Wherever your thoughts go, keep in mind that they are only thoughts. However, when allowing your thoughts to go wild during magic you must keep a close eye on the "when." It's fine for your mind to wander during the conjuring/building phase, but would not be so great when releasing the energy to do your bidding. It must be transformed before release.

It is easy to get carried away with an exercise of this nature and send it out to do your will instead of channeling it into a facility, so use every precaution.

Some people experience trouble with the type of sexual thoughts they have in Anger Magic. They feel guilty for letting themselves think such horrible things (and believe me, some of what may go through your mind can be truly shocking). Some may even wonder whether entertaining such thoughts means they are "that way." It is important to distinguish here the reality of what you are dealing with when you combine anger and sex. Both are explosive and hard to control. Both are free flowing and unbalanced when they cross over the planes. Sexual release is so unbalanced that it can be nigh impossible to perform any type of activity while undergoing it.

Don't beat yourself up for your thoughts; the reality is that the actual act would be a *far* different experience. When you combine sex and anger you may have some of the most intense imaginable experiences and the orgasm may be exceedingly strong. This is not because of your true perverted nature, but it is a result of combining two such powerful energies.

The whole point of a fantasy is to invoke a "taboo" sensation. Forbidden fruit is always delicious. Having taboo thoughts does not make you a pervert; acting on them (if they harm) does.

Fireball

If you are planning to use the anger for destruction there is no need to transform it and every reason not to. (Simply conjure it into a visualized fireball and hurl it at the item that represents what you wish to destroy.)

An odd thing that tends to happen to fireballs is a predisposition to burn blue upon first sight. Rest assured this is normal and desired.

Hold your hands about a foot apart. Visualize your anger taking the shape of a fiery ball, floating between your palms.

Watch it grow until all of your anger is focused into the ball. Begin to rotate it. It moves faster and faster, changing colors until it is blazing red. When it begins to spark, it is ready to be thrown.

The Burning Man

For this exercise, you will need to build a fire and have a poppet (doll) representing yourself nearby. Personalize the poppet with hair or bits of fingernail clippings. Cast your circle. The sample exercise below is performed with the intent of dissolving fat cells, but you may use it to affect any other area of your life. Build your anger and, using the touch method (the transfer of energy through touch), channel it through your right hand into the doll. When you are quite sure the anger is all in there, begin to program the doll with voice affirmations. Chant something along the lines of, "You will seek and destroy the extra fat in my body." Word the chant however you like, but make sure the mission is clear. Chant the verse at the doll until you reach a heightened state, you will know when you begin to feel dizzy. Upon reaching this state shout, "So it is done!" And throw the doll onto the fire. You may sit and watch until the doll is naught but ash if you like.

The Volcano

For this exercise, you will perform a visualization of your head as a volcano. By the force of your will, you will contain the lava and allow it only to run smoothly down the sides.

Close your eyes and "see" your neck begin to form the base of the crater. See it turn from smooth skin to brown and rocky, feel it begin to grow warm. Up the neck, the mountain extends; once it reaches your crown the lava pit is exposed. Hold to the visualization until you can see it thoroughly. Now you may call up your anger through the crater and see the lava begin to rise. If it erupts, relax: Know that you will gain control of it. Slowly allow the lava to stream down the mountain slopes. Continue with the imagery until you feel you have gained control. It may take a while as a volcano is explosive, but take your time and master the image.

This exercise can be tailored to suit your needs. You may choose to concentrate on seeing the lava rise, only to watch it sink back down. You may wish to allow it to blow violently. You might even want to allow it to remain in place and bubble and steam. Any of these is fine; most crucial is to emphasize being in control.

12. Angry Energy-Raising Techniques

This chapter assumes that you have no storage facility or readily available form of anger to draw from for magical use. Therefore, we will seek to build one from the ground up. There are several techniques to do this, for Anger Magic we primarily work with four: (1) aggressive music, (2) sex, (3) remembrance, and (4) current situation.

Aggressive Music

Let's begin with an overview of aggressive music as a tool to build angry energy. Like all of the practices in this book, it is recommended you perform the energy raisings within the confines of a sacred circle. Be sure to allow your thoughts the freedom of going where they choose during the building portion.

Aggressive music speaks to the soul. Not only can music soothe the savage beast, it can incite it. Aggressive music causes a vibration in the chest and stomach from its strong drumming and bass line rhythms. It is fast, it is loud, and it is hostile.

In the past, it was thought that violence and aggression in music was a form of venting and could not influence others. According to research published by the American Psychiatric Association, the opposite is true. In an experiment involving more than 500 college students, studies found that aggression in the lyrics increased aggressive thoughts and feelings. Which only proves what practitioners of Anger Magic have known all along, music can piss you off.

Heavy metal music covers dark topics in the lyrics but if you remove the lyrics and listen only to the music, you will still feel its aggression. The screaming of words on top of it just allows you the freedom to scream with it. It is our intention, for this exercise, to build the anger and incite a rage.

Aggressive music has its roots in tribal warfare; certain patterns of drumming were used to pump up warriors before a battle. The same sort of action takes place at sporting events today. The band plays aggressive music to spur the players and fans to greater emotional heights. At the movies, producers use music to elicit emotion. Music communicates to the soul.

To use music as a tool for raising energy, choose a song or several songs that make you feel a little angry. If you have never noticed before what effect music may have on your moods, take note of where your thoughts roam during which type of songs. If your thoughts are directed to a particularly frustrating event, like a fight with a friend or loved one during a particular song, that song may relate to anger for you. To be sure, mix it in with other types of music and play it in between them. Try to catch yourself by surprise. If each time you listen to it, your thoughts return to the frustrating or hostile variety, then that music is linked with anger and can be used as a draw for it.

Once you select your songs, you can play them continually in your circle, to begin the building process.

To determine the level of aggressiveness you are currently at, as you are building, keep in mind a knees, stomach, and head visualization. At a low level, you will feel the energy in your knees, and may wish to walk about the circle. Don't, it is not time yet. At a medium level, it will reach the stomach and just touch upon the bottom of the heart. You may find yourself wanting to talk. Don't, it is not time yet. At a high level, it has entered the head. You may find you wish to shout and get it out. Don't, it is not time yet.

Because we are in the process of building the emotion to an acceptable level for magic, we will have to fight the natural inclinations of the body to release the energy. Hence, we walk at level two instead of level one. We talk at level three instead of level two. We contain the emotion at level three as long as we possibly can before release.

Once you are at a medium level, allow yourself to move your body around with the music. Do not try to be flowing and graceful, try to be aggressive. But no matter how it expresses itself, just go with the flow and allow yourself to have a wild, free, savage dancing experience. Keep your breath flowing and do not move about so much that you tire yourself out and have to begin all over.

Once the anger reaches level three you may experience a ringing in your ears. Now you may talk or sing along or scream. Just keep your breath flowing. Allow it to build as long as you possibly can. Your heart may race, you may sweat, and things may go weird for a moment. Throw your head back and let it loose! Breathe it out, shout it out, push it out, it doesn't matter—just let it go. Direct it where you want it to go. It may be placed in a storage facility or a charm or whatever you want it to be placed in. This can be a wonderfully freeing exercise.

Sex

Let's move on to the overview of sexual energy raising. I am sure you remember the exercise in chapter 11 that teaches a release method using sex. The purpose in this technique is to not allow that release. That is correct, you are not allowed to reach an orgasm. Sound frustrating? It can be, but it works very well.

(If you are attempting this with a partner always make him or her aware of your purpose. Quite often, your partner may not want to participate, and I can't really find fault with that, because sex and anger are such a powerful combination. When you toss frustration into that mix, one can't help but wonder if it will get violent. You must remain in control at all times.)

Begin as if it were a normal sexual encounter. Once you feel yourself getting close to orgasm be sure to be the one in charge.

Continue with your activity until the last possible second before release and stop. Once the excitement has subsided and the possibility of orgasm has diminished, begin again. Continue until you get close to orgasm again and stop. Believe me, after doing this a few times you will start to become angry. Once the frustration becomes anger, you are not done. You are just getting started.

Keeping the knees, stomach, and head visualization in mind, continue with the start–stop series of actions until your frustration has reached the top of the head. This could take quite a bit of time, do not rush it. Once it has reached the top of the head, you will find yourself in a prime magical spot. If you have a spell set up or plans for the energy, you may now orgasm to release it for use. It is important to note here that we must not allow ourselves to be tricked by the body's need for release into orgasm too early. If the anger has not built to an appropriate level, we have gained nothing.

This is a building process, so we are fighting our body's natural urges for release. A partner usually has a tendency during exercises such as this to want you to release. For this reason, you must be the one dominating the activity.

If you choose to go it alone, then make certain you have the will-power to stop yourself before a climax. Be prepared to take your time with this and make certain you are assured of a lengthy privacy. Follow the guideline of the start–stop series of actions from the earlier example, and be strong.

Remembrance

The overview of remembrance as an anger building technique is simple and yet it is one of the hardest to perform correctly. Too often, we are hurt by the memories of hard things in our lives, and this is what spurs the anger, but we stop the memory process too soon from fear of opening old wounds.

If we are to use anger to heal ourselves, then we must allow ourselves to see the wound in its entirety. The same way a doctor cannot set a broken bone over the telephone, if we cannot face the whole memory we cannot work with it.

To begin this technique, write down on a piece of paper all of the times in your life when you felt you were being manipulated or purposely hurt. Include all of the times as a child when you felt frustrated and helpless. Add to that list the accidental hurts you have experienced. Once your list is fairly complete go back and add in the details of how you felt with each experience.

After you have completed that task, you should be sensing anger, if not outright fury. Pick the memory that makes you the most enraged or hurt and replay it in your mind, over and over. Keep in mind the knees, stomach, and head visualization and continue until you reach the head. You may find yourself crying, shaking, sweating or sick to your stomach—but carry on. If your intent is magical work, then you may use a release method and go about it. If your purpose is self-healing, read on.

Once you reach the head you may choose to enter the memory. It is yours; you can do what you want with it. Allow it to play in your mind like a movie and just walk in. Once you have entered the memory you may now do whatever it is you wish to do. You are in charge; you can change it to suit you. The only limit to this is your own imagination. When completing this exercise, it is nice to spoil yourself with some "you" time. Take a hot bath, eat ice cream; it doesn't matter, as long as you tend to your delicate child-like side.

Current Situation

The use of a current situation as an anger-building technique is complex and must be flexible and individual. By this I mean, if you are angry, and if you wish to use that anger immediately, you must have a harness in place.

A harness can be many things. It can be an enchanted necklace, a prism, or any favored trinket. You may have more than one, and you can keep them in various places about your home or on your person.

I personally have two. One is a screaming banshee doll on my computer desk leftover from Halloween. She is ugly, she is scary, and she looks mad. The feeling of anger within me becomes more pronounced when I grab her and squeeze her into screaming. It is as if she is calling my anger out.

Many little toys are marketed today as stress relievers and you can use one of those for anger-building purposes. Some look like little lumps of clay and you squeeze them to vent your frustrations into them. If you combine that with magical channeling of the energy into the item, you can use the lumps for storage or as building tools.

Clay works well as a harness. You can shape it into a statue or simply pound it. You can use paint or inks and create beautiful works of art as a harness. A particularly good harness is journaling.

And you might be a person who bakes, in which case you may employ your kitchen activities as stress relief. Anger does not fit well in the kitchen. The kitchen is a place for nurturing your family and their health. It is the heart of the home. If you frequently find yourself going to the kitchen for relief, you may wish to figure out a method of anger work that will not compromise your atmosphere. I suggest cleaning. It may sound silly and very mundane, but cleaning can harness your anger quite well.

Once you have your personal harness method figured out, you may begin to use it as a tool for building the anger. Once again, how you do that will depend on the object or task at hand.

13. Determining Your Best Form

No one quiz can hope to determine every nuance of an individual's personality. The function of the quiz below is not to tell you who I think you are according to the answers you provide. Rather, it is to help you assess who you think you are and to determine your best way to work with Anger Magic. The questions are personality based instead of magical or ethical. Some of them may seem like ethical quandaries, but try not to overthink your answers. Just try to answer the questions from your gut instinct and your first impression. Keep in mind there are no wrong answers. The test is only a tool to gauge your response pattern.

Four archetypes are provided, but they are merely the tip of the iceberg. You may identify equally with two or even three of them. Because of that possibility, I recommend retaking this quiz once a month and keeping track of the results. You may find yourself slowly gravitating toward one particular archetype, or you may find that over time you switch to another type entirely.

Read the following statements, then circle the letter you feel most applies to you.

1. You witness an act of violence. It is in small scale, a simple slap, but there is obvious trouble brewing. You:
   a. Step in between the two parties.
   b. Find out what instigated the slap.
   c. Stand and watch to see what happens next.
   d. Think to yourself, "That has to hurt."

2. Your boss is yelling at you for being late. You were caught in traffic due to a collision but he will not listen. You:

   a. Take a deep breath and stand firm. You make no comment and simply brace yourself for the onslaught.

   b. Wonder if there are mitigating circumstances you should be aware of that make it such a big deal.

   c. Stand with your head down and silently promise yourself it will never happen again.

   d. Twist your rings around your finger and wish he would hurry and finish.

3. You find yourself engaged in a squabble with a coworker. Outraged and out of control, he hits you. You:

   a. Stiffen your spine and grab his hands, preventing him from abusing you further.

   b. Wonder what in the world has happened to this person to make him so violent.

   c. Hold your cheek and report this person to higher-ups.

   d. Hit back; you are not going to let anyone abuse you!

4. A coworker takes the coffee money from the kitty at work knowing that you see her doing it. She has been with the company a lot longer than you have. She looks at you and laughs and states that it's only a few pennies. You:

   a. Yell at her that you are not a thief and will not stand by and watch her steal. If you did you may as well have stolen it yourself.

   b. Turn her in. Even if the bosses don't believe you, you are not willing to risk guilt by association.

   c. Tell her it is not too late to put it back and recommend she do so.

   d. Turn and leave, promising yourself that if anyone asks you will tell the truth.

5. You are at a party and spy someone else kissing your significant other. You:
   a. March right up to them and push the other person away.
   b. Walk over and say, "What is going on here?"
   c. Walk over and stare at them, waiting for them to notice that you see what they are doing.
   d. Grab someone else and kiss him or her. Why should your partner have all the fun?

6. Someone cuts you off in traffic. You:
   a. Ride their bumper and honk your horn.
   b. Think to yourself what an a—hole the driver is.
   c. Feel upset but do nothing.
   d. Yell out, "Have a great day! Hope you don't kill yourself!"

7. You are in a grocery store. You hear a small child crying and turn to see the mother spanking the child. You:
   a. Call the authorities.
   b. Walk over to the mother and ask what is going on.
   c. Give her an evil look and walk by.
   d. Demand she stop, now!

8. You are a cashier at a restaurant. You have never had a problem with your count being off at the end of the day. Today, however, you are exactly one hundred dollars off. The head cashier has been in the drawer several times that day. You know how many hundred-dollar bills were there, and one is missing. She is defending you to high heaven and insisting that the mistake will be found, but you know she took the money. You:
   a. Tell the manager immediately what you think and demand that you both be searched to prove it.

b. Wonder if perhaps it isn't an innocent mistake.
c. Say nothing, even though you are upset.
d. Confront the head cashier in private and tell her that
    you know she took it.

9. You have applied for a transfer to a less stressful position
    within your organization. You have worked there for three
    years and have an excellent record. The team hires an
    employee who has been with them for two months and has
    just graduated college. You:
    a. File a grievance.
    b. Speak to your supervisor about why and determine to
        try again.
    c. Say nothing and try harder.
    d. Give the new man a hard time to see if he can cut it.

10. A coworker schedules an appointment for you with a client
    and does not tell you about it. The coworker should have
    handled the issue herself instead of passing it on to you. You
    arrive at the office and find that the client has been waiting
    for you for thirty minutes. You:
    a. Write out a report about the incident.
    b. Ask the coworker why she did not do as she promised.
    c. Say nothing and continue on as usual.
    d. Take charge, apologize to the client for the mistake,
        and get to work.

If your answers were mostly *A*'s you will work well as a warrior
in Anger Magic. You take action and chances. You know you may
be wrong and yet you still risk it for the sake of doing the right
thing. You are disciplined and fearless. You believe in holding
people accountable for their actions, including yourself. You can be
a bit hasty and overly critical of others. You do not go looking for
fights, but if you stumble across a challenge, you rise to the occasion.

You despise weakness and have a tendency to be perceived as rigid. Warrior types relate well to the element of Fire. Traits to be aware of that commonly fall in this group include bullying behavior, savage tendencies, power tripping, and out-of-control addictions.

If your answers were mostly *B*'s you will work well in a justice capacity. You always consider mitigating circumstances and your natural curiosity insists that you know all of the facts before reaching any conclusion. Because you consider all sides of a situation, you may be slow to action, but when you get around to it you are rarely wrong. Your friends usually consider you to be extremely fair and wise. Judge types relate well to the element of Water. Traits to be aware of that commonly fall into this category are a propensity to dictatorship, unbalanced emotions, and overly judgmental attitudes.

If you answered with mostly *C*'s you are of a more traditional type. You will do best to use the power of Anger Magic in your personal life or the world immediately around you. You are nurturing and loving. You normally avoid fighting but when you do decide to duke it out people stop and listen. Your words hold weight. You are well balanced and grounded yet you may need to frequently purge the extra emotions. Traditional types relate best to the element of Earth. Traits to be aware of that commonly belong to this group include the tendency to martyrdom, and to seeing oneself as a victim.

If you answered mostly *D*'s you are a true free thinker! Independent and strong, you tend to be a bit impulsive. You can work with Anger Magic in any capacity as long as you slow down first. The unique aspect of a free thinker is that at any time you may flow from one type to another—indeed you hold them all inside. The wonderful thing about you is your ability to put yourself in another's situation so accurately. Freethinking types relate well to the element of Air. Traits to be aware of that commonly belong to this group are jealousy, rebellious behavior, and a tendency to see yourself as a victim.

Each of these types are based on your personality *before* utilizing the system of Anger Magic. Predestination toward one type is by no means indicative of the only way for you to work with Anger Magic. It is simply a starting point to consider.

If you have an equal number of answers from more than one type, merge them, consider the combination, and go from there.

14. Meditations

editation can help us to discover our anger bases. By "anger bases" I mean the source of our anger, what our obstacles are, where our anger originated, and what is the best use of it.

Meditation also helps flush out the perception of stress and resulting bodily tensions, which are key factors in uncontrolled anger. Meditation also teaches you to focus your attention and control your mind. Meditation clears your chakras of blockages, allowing you to maintain a greater connection to spirit in your daily life. It reprograms the "hot buttons" you may have as it heals the body, mind, and soul's energies.

There is no wrong way to meditate. But there are a few things that are considered detrimental. Meditation does not work well if you are hungry. Hunger pangs are distracting. If you eat a light snack beforehand, it will be easier to focus your attention. Furthermore, don't try to force it. Meditation requires a conscious relaxation of thought patterns. If you are busy fighting off thoughts, you are not free to drift.

I recommend recording the meditation transcribed below on a cassette tape for easier use. When recording speak with a slow, steady rhythm and a relaxed voice. Make sure to allow enough room on the tape for the pauses, for it is then that your mind will be forming the imagery. Once you are ready to perform the meditation, simply start the tape.

The Red Sea

The goal of this meditation is to meet with—and embrace—your shadow side.

To prepare for the Red Sea Meditation, it is best to seat yourself comfortably. Place pillows on the floor of your sacred space so you will have somewhere to recline.

Prepare an altar; light a musky-type incense and a small candle. If you are thirsty, sipping herbal tea is nice. Smudge the area with sage and cast a circle.

Light your incense, focus on the altar, and take a few deep, cleansing breaths. Say something along the lines of, "I have a shadow side, she is here with me. Tonight we meet at last. As I begin to know more of her, I begin to know more of myself." Start the tape.

Transcript for recording: Take a few deep breaths and connect yourself to the Earth. Ground deeply. *(long pause)* Close your eyes. There is darkness all around you; it is warm and comforting. Let the warmth wrap around you and allow yourself to be held by the night. *(long pause)* Ahead of you is a rocky cave that casts out a dim light. Walk to it. The coolness of the cave invites you in. Enter it. *(pause)* The softly lit cave opens upon a shoreline. The moon is full and bright. The aroma of the sea is strong and salty. Walk to the seaside. You see that the seawater is red. *(pause)* Put your toes in the water and allow the sea to lap at them. The feeling tickles and the water is surprisingly warm. *(pause)* You look across the horizon, and on the opposite shore you spy another cave. There is a woman walking out of it to the shoreline. She smiles and waves at you. *(long pause)* She stretches out her glossy black wings and begins to fly across the water to you. *(pause)* She lands gracefully a few feet from you. She is strikingly beautiful. *(pause)* Together the two of you stand while the sea begins to churn. *(pause)* The wind begins to whip your hair about your head. You ask the woman, "Who are you?" *(pause)* She answers, in a voice strong and power-ful, "I am your dark mother. It is I who guide you through the night. It is I who hold you tight in my arms. I am your life, I am your death, and I am you." *(long pause)* She takes your hand and leads you into the warm, red water. "Do you feel the water's warmth, child?" she asks. You do and so you nod. *(pause)* She answers, "It is warm from the life it once was. For this water is of blood. The blood of all life come before and all life yet to be." *(long pause)* Reach down and cup your hands, scoop up a handful of the red water. It sparkles under the moonlight. *(pause)* The dark mother whispers to you and shows you all about creation and death that you wish to know. *(long pause)* When you have heard all you wish to know, you find yourself in her arms. *(pause)* She embraces and blesses you and you prepare to leave. *(pause)* You turn and walk back toward the entrance to the cave. *(pause)* You walk into the coolness of the cave and stroll slowly to the other side, where you came from. *(pause)* You reflect upon your words with the mother. *(pause)* You walk out of the cave and are back in your body. Right here and now. Take a deep breath and slowly stretch your body back into full awakening. [*End of transcript.*]

Write down your experiences in a meditation journal. Thank the dark mother for showing you what you needed to see. Close circle.

Storm Surge

The goal of this meditation is discovering where your anger stems from and how strong it is. Recognition is key to creating a harness. A harness is used to train the emotion to follow your bidding.

Set an altar with a blue, a yellow, and a black candle. Find a rain-scented incense to burn. If you can add wind blowing on your face via a fan, do so. Be careful not to point the air at the flames. Scatter pillows around so you can get comfortable. Cast circle.

Settle yourself among the pillows on the floor. Light the incense and the candles. Focus on your altar. Let your vision blur. Start the tape.

Transcript for recording: Breathe deeply. Feel your connection to the Earth. *(pause)* Allow yourself to grow roots that reach deep within the Earth. *(long pause)* Close your eyes. You are walking down a moonlit path. *(pause)* Before you is a cool, dimly lit cavern. You walk through the entrance and follow a sandy path. *(pause)* You emerge on the other side of the cave. You find yourself standing on a sandy beach. The sky is bright and clear. The sun is shining. *(pause)* You smell the salty water and hear the birds singing. You feel refreshed. *(pause)* You look to the East and see a small dark cloud forming. *(pause)* It is moving closer and closer. *(pause)* You see the cloud growing. Larger and larger it churns itself into a cloud big enough to dim the sky. *(long pause)* The wind starts to blow and your hair is flying about. *(pause)* Lightning starts to flash brightly in the sky and thunder rolls. *(long pause)* You begin to turn with the wind to your left. *(pause)* Faster and faster, you twirl about until the bottom half of you forms a tornado. *(long pause)* You rise to the top of the darkest cloud and peek inside. *(pause)* Before you, you see churning raw emotions that are black. *(pause)* One by one, you identify the emotions. *(long pause)* As you call the name of the emotion, it dissipates into the power of your tornado. You now own it. *(long pause)* Take your time and identify as many emotions as you wish. *(long pause)* When you are finished and have identified all that you wish to, the tornado half of you begins to slow and lower you below the clouds. You find yourself planted firmly on the sandy beach once more. *(pause)* You look at the cloud and notice it has changed. The color is different. The size is smaller. *(pause)* The sun begins to burn brightly once more. *(pause)* Your body is warm and you sit on the sand to rest. *(pause)* You close your eyes. *(pause)* You open your eyes and find yourself back in your body, right here. Right now. *(pause)* Stretch slowly and feel the comforting weight of your body. [*End of transcript.*]

Take a few cleansing breaths and write down in your journal what emotions you found and how the cloud changed once you acknowledged them. Log how you are feeling now. Close circle.

Each time you do this meditation, you will gain confidence and understanding of how anger works in the human senses. Recognition is a gradual process, so do not overdo it and meet all of your anger stems at once. I recommend doing this meditation once or twice a month, but no more than that—or you may feel overwhelmed by the emotional weight.

The Morrighan Meditation

The goal of the Morrighan Meditation is preparation. The Morrighan was a methodical goddess and will help put emotions and goals in a logical order so you can prepare for magical work. In case you have a large amount of anger and are not sure where to best use it, Morrighan can help.

Meeting the Morrighan is not an easy task and should not be taken lightly.

To prepare, set up an altar with a cauldron of ice and water and light three red floating candles inside it. Place a black raven feather on the altar. Light sandalwood incense. Cast circle in your usual manner.

Scatter pillows around your meditation area so you have somewhere comfortable to recline and relax. Settle yourself among the pillows and breathe deeply.

Transcript for recording: Feel your body begin to relax. *(pause)* Relax your fingers, your hands, and your arms. *(pause)* Relax your toes, your feet, and your legs. *(pause)* Relax your back and stomach. *(pause)* Relax your chest and neck. *(pause)* Relax your face and close your eyes. *(pause)* Feel your whole body settle deeper into a state of total relaxation. *(pause)* Let the worries of the day just float away. *(pause)* Take a deep breath and slowly exhale. *(pause)* You find yourself on a riverbank surrounded by a lush green forest. *(pause)* You hear birds singing and smell the crisp fresh smell of pine trees. *(pause)* Without thinking about it you begin to follow the river, walking along the side of the water, relaxed and happy. You are enjoying the sunshine on your shoulders. *(long pause)* You come to the river bend and see a rocky formation jutting from the water. *(pause)* You watch—mesmerized—noting how the current flows around the rocks and listening to the melodious song the water sings. *(long pause)* You look to your left and see an old woman washing clothing on another rock formation. *(pause)* As you watch her she grows a bit taller, her hair changes from gray to a long luxurious black. *(pause)* She stands tall, turns to you, and smiles. It is a smile of welcome and safety. *(pause)* She walks over to you and introduces herself warmly as Morrighan. *(pause)* You recognize her as a warrior queen and are unsure how to respond. Morrighan notices this and to put you completely at ease she embraces you in a warm hug. *(pause)* She whispers to you the secrets of order and continuity. She gives you sacred insight on how to follow a logical pattern of action with your emotions. *(long pause)* After you have heard all you wish to hear She whispers good-bye to you, for now. *(pause)* You turn and follow the river back from where you came. *(pause)* Upon reaching the warm sunny spot where you began the journey, you sit down to rest for a moment. *(pause)* You close your eyes and enjoy the warmth of the sun upon your face. *(pause)* You open your eyes and are back in your body, right here, right now. [*End of transcript.*]

Make sure to record your journey in your meditation notebook before you close the circle.

The Willow

The goal of the Willow Meditation is chakra clearing and identification of past anger.

Arrange your meditation area as you normally do. Set an altar with a green candle and herbal incense. Settle your body among the pillows and relax. Cast circle.

Transcript for recording: Close your eyes and become as calm and comfortable as you can. *(pause)* Lay your hands in your lap, fingers straight, and palms up. *(pause)* The tips of your middle fingers are almost touching. *(pause)* Focus on your root chakra. As you see it, it changes from a clear red to a willow seed surrounded by clear red. *(pause)* Take three deep breaths. *(pause)* You hear your heart beating and with the exhale you see a strong trunk emerge from the seed. *(pause)* It stops at your sacral chakra. It builds the sacral chakra to a clear bright orange, then bursts through it on a path to the next one. As the trunk continues straight up it has many branches stemming all through your body. *(pause)* Take three deep breaths. *(pause)* The trunk reaches your solar plexus. *(pause)* You see the chakra swell and it is a bright clear yellow; the trunk bursts through and spreads more branches throughout your body. *(pause)* The trunk reaches your heart chakra. *(pause)* It fills the chakra with energy and it turns a beautiful clear pink before it bursts through and spreads its branches throughout you. *(pause)* You see the trunk grow to your throat chakra and energize it with a clear bright blue before popping through. *(pause)* You see the trunk growing thinner and know the tree is almost complete. *(pause)* The trunk grows to your third eye and energizes it with a violet light. It is clear and glowing. The trunk continues to your crown chakra. *(pause)* At the crown chakra, the trunk blossoms into a full-blown willow tree. Your crown chakra glows with a warm white light and the branches of the tree hold you close in an embrace. *(pause)* You are at one with the willow. You feel the woody texture of the limbs and smell the willow's fragrance. *(pause)* You look at your leaves. *(pause)* There is something written on them. You look closer. *(pause)* You see that the leaves are covered with examples of times in your life when you were angry. *(pause)* You examine one of the leaves closely, knowing that you may, at any time, choose another. *(pause)* You read as many leaves as you wish. *(pause)* After reading them, the leaves gently float away on the wind. *(pause)* That anger has left you. *(pause)* When you have finished reading your leaves, you feel the branches pull back into themselves. *(pause)* One by one, chakra by chakra, the willow retreats until another time. *(pause)* When it is back to a seed you realize you are in your body, right here and now. Take three deep, cleansing breaths. [*End of transcript.*]

Write down in your journal what leaves you read and what experiences you had. Close circle.

It is entirely up to you whether you wish to allow the anger to float away or save it for magical use. Many times, there will not be much power left in the original anger to save, but if it is important to you, you may save and store it. Simply remove the float away option when you record the tape.

Take as long as you need with this meditation. If you feel that you did not identify enough of your past anger, lengthen your pauses and keep going the next time you do it.

III. Mastering the Magic

Deities, Myths, and Correspondences

15. Kali-Ma

When Kali-Ma, the great Hindu goddess with the terrifying visage, dances, the world trembles. There is no power like that of Kali-Ma, the Black Mother. She holds within herself the key to all destruction and resurrection. Kali-Ma is the epitome of life cycles, representing death to allow for the passing of the old, and birth to welcome the new.

There are many descriptions of the creation, purpose, and worship of Kali-Ma. The one I present here is mine. Kali has been long known to appear to whom she wants; however she wants. Therefore, interpretation and experience of Kali is completely individual.

Kali is said to have emanated from the brow of the great goddess Durga (the slayer of demons) during a battle between divine and anti-divine forces. She is considered to be a forceful form of Durga.

Kali is usually depicted as a blue or black woman with four arms. In one hand she holds a sword. In another, she holds the head of a slain demon. With her other two arms, she encourages her worshippers. She wears earrings composed of dead bodies (said to be young boys) and a necklace of skulls. The only form of clothing she wears is a belt made from the arms of men. Her tongue (often said to be black when she is depicted as a blue woman) protrudes from her mouth to her chin. Her three eyes are red and her face and chest are often covered with blood. She has long black hair that is matted with blood and hangs to her feet. In one of her most popular depictions, she squats over her consort Shiva and is copulating with him and consuming his bowels at the same time. Kali can be pretty terrifying to view.

When Kali is depicted as black and called the Black Mother, it is to symbolize her transcendence of all levels of life, time, and space. Black is the absence of color, and all colors disappear within black. Such is Kali. She is all things and all levels.

Kali is depicted as nude to symbolize truth. She is the embodiment of spirit. Her disheveled hair represents the fabric of space and time.

The belt of arms represents karma. The thought behind this is that man cannot commit transgressions against other men if he has no arms. The necklace of skulls represents knowledge. Her protruding tongue symbolizes nature in all of its flavors and her consumption of all. Her four arms represent a complete cycle of creation and destruction, and denotes the fact that she contains all this. Her three eyes symbolize that she sees into the past, present, and future.

The name Kali is the feminine form of *kala*, which is the Sanskrit word for time. However, Kali is not time, she is the power behind time, which devours all things. One of her purposes is to let us know our time on Earth is limited. She reminds us that refusing to think about our own deaths and destruction is merely wrapping ourselves in an illusion. As human beings, our time *is* limited.

Kali is a protector of humans; she is our mother. She slays the demons of this world. It is she who rids the world of ignorance and ego. In one legend, her followers were attempting to perform a human sacrifice in her honor. Enraged by this, Kali jumped out from the altar and decapitated them with their own sword. She is fiercely protective of the innocent. (The darker path of Kali worship asserts that she was enraged because her followers had attempted to sacrifice a female to her, since only males are considered suitable sacrificial offerings.)

The demon Raktaviga attacked Kali. She was amused at this at first, until she found that with each drop of blood he lost, thousands more demons sprang up. This, too, enraged her. Soon there were so many demons that even Shiva, who watched from his fire circle where he maintained world order, wondered if Kali would survive. Therefore, Kali licked up the demon blood and the demons were unleashed within her, where they were destroyed by her immortal essence. This made Kali even stronger and soon Raktaviga lay dead at her feet.

She began to dance upon his body. She became so caught up in the dance that as she whirled with fury, the Earth began to tremble. Her dance was shaking the world's order.

Kali-Ma's dance formed a perfect circle and legend states that in order to stop her from destroying the Earth the great lord Shiva threw himself under her feet so that man might live a while longer. When Kali recognized she was dancing upon her husband's body instead of that of the demon, she immediately stopped. She lovingly cleaned him, apologized, and placed him back in his ring of fire to bring the world back to order. The legend goes on to state that there will come a day when Shiva will not stop her dance, and it will end the world.

There is no avoiding Kali. She marks the eternal change that is life. She is the very force behind it. Acceptance of Kali will bring her many blessings into your life. While Kali-Ma may seem terrifying, she is natural and benevolent.

Historically some forms of her worship have been a bit grim by Western standards (and some still are today). According to some sources, working with Kali offers unique opportunities in magic. It is said that Kali holds secrets of certain magical powers.

These powers are reputed to include astral journeys, resurrection, possession of another's body, the ability to see through physical obstacles, flying, and the ability to make a weapon invincible. These are thought to be part of a lefthand path of Kali worship. The rituals required to produce these powers appear exceedingly dark to our Western eyes. Often they involve ritual sex, an overabundance of mind-altering drugs, the procurement and abuse of corpses, and animal sacrifice. Obviously, these things can be obstacles to working with Kali. It is intimidating to know that while others are worshipping her in such strong ways we do relatively tame things such as offer a glass of cool water to quench her thirst.

It is extremely important to note that Kali is essentially a mother and a creator. There is no reason we cannot worship and work with that aspect of her. We do not have to focus on her dark side to know her, and we never have to perform activities such as those mentioned above to make our work with her valid.

We do have to be aware of such activities though. There are reasons dark worship of Kali exists, and hiding from the truth of it will only gain her laughter at us. In this life, there is the good, the bad, and the ugly. Working with Kali requires acknowledging them all. She allows for no shielding from the truth.

However, we need not be intimidated by the darker aspects of Kali worship; worship of Kali in a benign form can be quite beautiful and spiritually satisfying.

Puja is an ancient system of Kali worship. It includes powerful Tantric methods of devotion. It begins with sipping water that has been charged with the holy name of Kali in order to purify the mouth and prepare it to chant. Then the water is used to cleanse the space around the worshipper. The holy water is sprinkled about offerings, fresh flowers, and the worshipper's tools to further purify all things involved. The practitioner visualizes a ring of fire around them and chanting begins in order to invoke the mother into the heart.

Once Kali is in the heart, worship begins, and this traditionally includes sixteen offerings for Kali.

1. She is offered a seat.
2. She is offered a prayer of welcome.
3. Her feet are washed.
4. Respect is shown by offering flowers or leaves.
5. She is given a glass of cool water.

6. She is offered a special ritual dish of worship, which includes milk, yogurt, honey, sugar water, and ghee.

7. She is offered water for washing the mouth.

8. She is given a bath.

9. She is offered new clothing.

10. She is gifted with jewelry.

11. She is offered perfume.

12. She is given fresh flowers.

13. Incense is lit in her honor and to please her.

14. A candle is lit to provide her with light.

15. She is given food.

16. She is honored with prayers.

The ritual ends with a waving of lights. Typically, the worshipper would take a lit candle and wave it gently in the air to light her way and say farewell for now.

Kali is said to dwell on cremation sites. In India, traditional funeral rites are cremations. The five elements of life are dissolved in the cremation process. Kali is thought to be the very pyre to help burn away the limits of the human body. She is there to crush the human ego, which is thought to reside in the flesh. Some gather to worship her on the cremation grounds; others choose to do so in a temple or other place they hold sacred. If you call upon Kali from the heart, it will not matter where you call from, she will hear and she will answer.

Kali transcends the labels of man. She is both good and bad, she is all. According to Tantric teachings the world over, Kali is viewed in the same light as fire. While it can burn you, it can also warm you.

Kali is said to bestow upon her devotees a special mantra used in ritualistic sex magic. It is said that this mantra is the secret to performing successful magic and that you must never—even on pain of death—reveal it. The secret of all paths of Kali worship comes down to that one small detail. Hold the mantra she gifts you with as pure and use it to stay in contact with her. It is your private link to her and you must cherish it.

So how does Kali relate to Anger Magic? She reinforces the existence of anger as a purpose. Though it can be terrible to behold, it is necessary as a force.

She reminds us that many times destruction is a good thing. Kali shows us that with her slaying of demons.

She also reminds us not to get too caught up in our emotions, specifically anger. As she became so wrapped up in her dance, she almost destroyed the world. She helps us to understand that the trials and confusion borne of dealing with anger exist only on this plane.

Correspondences

Symbols: an hourglass, fire
Colors: red, blue, black
Lunar phase: the crescent moon
Animals: black cats, hawks, crows, elephants
Affinities: skull-shaped objects, necklaces, swords, conch shells, offerings of cool water
Flora: fresh flowers
Purposes: purification, magic, to unbind something, transformations, time spells

16. Hecate

The goddess Hecate is native to ancient Thrace. She was both a lunar goddess and the goddess of the Underworld. Her name means "she who works from afar" and was meant to be a parallel of Apollo's title of the "far-darter."

According to Hesiod, Hecate was the daughter of the Titans Asteria and Perses. In later myths she is said to have been the daughter of Zeus and Hera. This misconception is due to the fact that she helped the Olympians overthrow the Titans during their famous war.

Because she helped Zeus in his war effort against the Titans, he honored her above all other goddesses. She was the only Titan to retain any powers after the Olympian gods began their rule. Zeus gave her the Underworld to rule and also the Earth and sky. He called upon her to help rescue his daughter Persephone, and she was successful.

No discussion of Hecate would be complete without touching on the myth of Persephone, one explanation of the seasons of the year. Demeter had born a child of Zeus named Persephone. One day Hades stumbled upon Persephone at play in a field and fell in love with her. He grabbed her up and took her to the Underworld with him to become his wife. No one heard her screams except for Hecate and Helios.

For nine days, Demeter searched for her beloved daughter to no avail. Even the gods upon Olympus would not tell her what had happened to her child. Hecate went to Demeter and told her she had heard Persephone screaming from her cave. She did not tell her why she screamed but only suggested that Demeter ask

Helios. Heartbroken, Demeter continued to search the entire Earth for her child and was inconsolable when she could not find her.

Finally Demeter went to Helios. Upon asking him, she discovered that Hades had abducted her child. She left Olympus and forsook her duties and determined to remain in exile until her daughter was returned.

Demeter was the goddess of grains, and she therefore held the world's fertility in her hands. Her self-imposed exile caused a barren winter state to fall upon the Earth. Zeus, who maintained order on Earth, insisted that his brother Hades return Persephone so that the Earth might become fruitful again. Zeus did not know that Persephone had eaten seven pomegranate seeds, which bound her to remain with Hades.

As a sort of compromise, during the fall and winter seasons Persephone would remain in the Underworld with her husband Hades and the Earth would be barren. In the spring and summer seasons she would return to her mother, Demeter, who in her happiness made the world fruitful again.

Hecate is considered part of a trinity thought to include Demeter as crone and Persephone as mother (however, these aspects are heavily debated). This trio of goddesses is perhaps the earliest merging of deities from which the triple goddess myths evolved. She is often thought to be the crone when in fact, Hecate is a maiden. As the origins of her myths are Greek, we do not see Hecate depicted as a crone until later, when the Roman myths begin to evolve. Hecate is often shown as having three heads, many times they are not human. She is the ruler of the Underworld and also rules the Earth and sky.

It is believed Hecate's consort was the god Hermes; it is with him that she is said to lead the Wild Hunt. In Greek myths the Wild Hunt has Hecate roaming the Earth at night with a pack of black dogs searching for lost souls to guide.

Hecate had two daughters, Scylla and Circe—both were Witches. Scylla was the product of a union between Hecate and

Phorcys. Circe was the child of Hermes, as well as Medea's aunt. Medea was a high priestess for Hecate.

Hecate came to be known as a goddess of childbirth. Myths show her fleeing from her mother, because her mother was angry that Hecate had stolen her rouge and given it to Europa. Hecate ran to the home of a woman who had recently given birth. As Hecate had contact with the child and mother, it was thought to have made her impure. She plunged the child into a fire to purify him and went in with him to guard him from harm.

In later myths, the legends change and she acquired a darker side. Hecate was thought to be a demon as well as a goddess of Witchcraft, "black" magic, and evil. She was said to be the mother of a group of vampire demon goddesses called the Empusae, who lured young men into their beds and killed them, afterward feeding upon their carcasses.

Hecate is quite often feared by those who do not understand her. She was a nurturer to the young, an empress, and a queen. Hecate comforted as well as punished when necessary. Hecate was originally a goddess of fertility by day and restored life to failed crops. By night, she was affiliated with Witchcraft and ghosts. She was the goddess of the storms and was thought to eradicate crops when displeased.

Because she combined the aspects of life with death and rebirth, perhaps people uncomfortably speculated on Hecate's dark side and grew to fear her. Gradually she came to be seen as a dark goddess and an all-powerful Witch. It is important to note here that it was with this shift in emphasis that the number of her worshippers *increased*.

Sacrifices that were made to Hecate included black female sheep, black dogs, and black bulls. Evidence has been found that suggests devotees of Hecate participated in curses and negative magic.

Hecate has many incarnations that are specific to a task. Here are some of them:

Hecate Trivia was the goddess of the crossroads. Trivia guided those who needed it, meeting them at the crossroads and telling them the correct path to take.

Hecate Propolos was also a guide, one that guided the soul through transformations. She also guided soul transformation on Malkuth.

Hecate Propylaia—which translates to "before the doors"—is the guardian of entryways. She protects the home and temple.

Hecate Phosphorous—or light bearer—is symbolic of Hecate leading lost souls through the darkness to a restful place to await rebirth.

Hecate Kourotrophos is the protector of children and childbirth.

Hecate Chthonia—which means "of the Earth"—is an aspect of Hecate's that is powerful for banishing work, as she knows all of the Earth's mysteries. It is she who seeks the departed souls to lead them into the underworld.

Hecate had two black hounds that were said to have served her. Their original function was to accompany Hecate through graveyards and sniff out any souls that needed her guidance. They were later twisted into the myths of the "hellhound." Hecate was thought to have ruled over all wild animals. It is in the aspect of animal goddess that Hecate was sometimes depicted as an animal. Her voice was sometimes said to be like that of a howling dog or a bellowing bull.

Hecate was said to control serpents, and in later myths her hair was made of snakes. In this aspect, she can be seen to control the psychosexual energy symbolically represented by serpents.

Hecate's mysteries included knowledge of time and how to control it, menstruation, and fertility. Her teachings indicate that these things can all be mastered on the inner planes.

Hecate also symbolized the spectrum of birth, sex, death, and rebirth—the never-ending cycle of life. As a living flame, Hecate is the embodiment of a soul seeker: Carrying two torches and wearing a headdress of stars, she searches the dark realms to salvage lost souls and lead them to a place of rest and rebirth.

Hecate can help us to look inside and find our own darkness. She is our soul's guide to rest and preparation for rebirth.

Shrines for Hecate are often placed either right outside the entry to one's home or immediately inside it so that she may guide and protect the visitor. Hecate shrines—in the capacity of guardian—were often found in the temples and sanctuaries of other deities. This shows how important she is in her role as protector and guide. Because she is needed in that capacity to guide one through another deity's temple.

Pagans the world over still worship Hecate; her mythology continues to grow as we add our modern-day interpretations to the available ancient scripts. She is associated with healing, especially of psychological hurt.

While Hecate has been demonized by the Catholic Church and portrayed as sinister in the plays of William Shakespeare, working with her need not be feared. She is wise and powerful but not at all overbearing or controlling.

Correspondences: As Hecate rules the Earth, sky, and Underworld she relates to Earth, Air, and Spirit. Hecate visits us in dreams and in storms, she is primal and uncontained. Because she is eternal and exists in all things, correspondences differ. I will list only the most common and encourage you to seek inside what she wishes you to use to connect with her.

Hecate faces the three-way crossroads and can see the past, present and future. Because of this, working with her is particularly effective for divination and psychic work.

Lunar phase: Any lunar phase is correct. Hecate is a moon goddess; specifically important to her myths are her associations with the dark and waning moon. However, it is appropriate to call upon Hecate at any moon phase.

Season: Hecate is often seen as an autumn and winter goddess.

Planet: Saturn

Stones: jet, onyx, hematite, smoky quartz, black obsidian

Colors: black, red, silver, gray, navy, purple

Trees: yew, willow, black poplar

Herbs: belladonna, azalea, aconite, mandrake, sandalwood, patchouli, lavender, hemlock, wolf bane, mugwort, hellebore, poppy, camphor, dandelion

Animals: snake, dogs, bulls, ravens, owls

Purposes: justice, power, transformation, illumination, protection, fertility, banishing, dream work, spell work, to increase psychic powers, scrying, healing, soul journeys

Numbers: 3, 9

Special days: November 16 is Hecate's night, a time to honor her. August 13 is the day to ask Hecate's blessing on forthcoming crops; as goddess of storms, she can wipe out entire crops. November 30 is the day of Hecate at the crossroads. Once a month on the thirtieth day, it is appropriate to worship her and offer a supper. It is also proper to cleanse your home at that time. Samhain is also a special day for Hecate.

Affinities: Hecate's suppers consist of offerings from the following foods: raw eggs, cheese, garlic, honey, bread, red mullet, mushrooms, and cake.

Symbols: keys, which represent the key to the soul and introspection; *rope,* which represents the tie between the soul, the astral planes, and the conscious; *the torch,* which represents the illuminations, her mysteries present;

a Greek cross; *the dagger*, which represents the cutting of the umbilical cord from birth and also the cord, which binds us to Malkuth, to set us free for rebirth.

The above list is only a starting point, there is no wrong lunar time to invoke or call Hecate and no wrong task, as she is the goddess of magic.

17. Pele

The beautiful Pele is the Hawaiian volcano goddess known as "she who shapes the land." She is passionate and volatile, the essence of fire in nature, the goddess of violence. She is also thought to control lightning. She loves hard, plays hard, angers easily, and lives to please herself first and foremost.

According to legend, Pele was quite the little minx. She seduced her sister Na-maka-o-kah'i's husband and ran away to hide from her fury. She settled in Mount Kilauea because it was the only place high enough to keep her fires from being drowned out by the huge waves sent by her wronged sister. Pele took many lovers and only a very few escaped with their lives. When she was angry with her lovers, she would hurl lava at them, transforming them into misshapen pillars of stone. These stones still dot the Hawaiian volcanic fields today.

One of her lovers, Kamapua'a, proved a match for the fiery Pele. Kamapua'a was a god of agriculture, a pig god, who wore a cape to hide the bristles on his back. Over the course of their battles, Pele would become angry and cover the land with molten lava. To retaliate Kamapua'a would send torrents of rain to extinguish the fires. Pele's brothers called off the war between them for fear that the land would become so waterlogged it would never be able to sustain fire again. Pele gave in to Kamapua'a and at a spot in Puna, the two became lovers. The passionate Pele and Kamapua'a shared company until a child was born, and then Pele went back to her philandering ways.

Pele's greatest rival is Poliahu, one of a group of four goddesses known chiefly as the goddesses of snow-capped mountains. Poliahu was a great beauty and seduced human chiefs. Pele epitomizes sexual feelings and is a very jealous goddess. This jealousy encouraged her rivalry with Poliahu to thrive. It is sometimes thought that their battle of "fire and ice" is still in progress today.

Pele's jealousy spills over to other areas of her life; she does not like to be bested. Legend has it that she was defeated in a sled race by a human chieftain and sent lava in her wake to consume him. He escaped, but narrowly.

Her uncontrolled jealousy also cost her a lover and almost a sister: According to this legend, Pele assumed mortal form and had an affair with Lohiau, a young hula dancer. She spent three days of bliss with him before deciding to go back to her home on Mount Kilauea. She promised Lohiau she would send for him, and she entrusted her sister Hiiaka with the task of bringing Lohiau to her. Hiiaka promised she would bring him if Pele would tend her gardens in exchange while she was gone. Hiiaka ran into a few problems and took longer than expected to reach the young man. By the time she got to him, Lohiau was dying from a broken heart, pining away for Pele. As he took what would have been his final breath, Hiiaka, never one to go back on a promise, forced his spirit back into his body and saved his life. She went forward on her task with the young man in tow.

In the meantime, Pele grew jealous thinking that because it was taking so long the two must be betraying her in body and heart. Her anger shook the Earth and she sent forth great clouds of black smoke. Hiiaka knew what this meant: Pele was angry.

Lohiau professed to loving Hiiaka more than Pele, but Hiiaka would not hear of it and determined to keep her promise and deliver him to Pele. When she arrived, she saw that Pele had not kept to her end of the bargain and in her jealousy had scorched and burned Hiiaka's gardens.

In revenge, Hiiaka threw herself upon Lohiau and made love to him on the edge of the volcano. Upon seeing this Pele sent forth red-hot, molten lava, which killed Lohiau instantly, but she could not harm her immortal sister. Hiiaka refused to accept defeat and went down into the bowels of the Earth to rescue the spirit of her new lover. She returned with him at the time of the arrival of Lohiau's best friend. Pele, lustful as she is, accepted the friend in exchange and allowed her sister and Lohiau to go forth and live in peace.

Pele had a benevolent side, too. Another legend tells of Pele—disguised as an old woman—walking on a mountain and spying two sisters cooking dinner for their family. Pele tells them she is hungry and has not eaten all day. The older sister selfishly refuses to share. The younger sister sat the old woman down in front of their fire and gave her some food. The older sister tried to stop her, but finally, there was no more food. The old lady stood up and prepared to leave. She turned to the younger sister and told her bad things were going to happen and that she should wrap a tapa around her home. The girl told her parents what had happened and sure enough, the volcano erupted that night. Everything was destroyed except the young girls' home and family.

Pele dwells in the craters of Mount Kilauea and sends molten lava down its slopes to increase land mass; as she destroys, she also creates. There is also a triple goddess aspect to the legends of Pele. She is said to appear to people up to this day as a child, a beautiful, passionate maiden, or an old crone. Interestingly, when the crone image appears in her myths, it is said that Pele is actually asleep. According to the ancient Hawaiians, sleep brought out the old hag she actually was. The image of Pele as a young beautiful maiden was a projection from her that stemmed from her jealous nature.

Many of the Hawaiian gods of old have been forgotten, but Pele worship still thrives today. People pay her homage by bringing offerings of cooked chicken and rum to throw into the crater of Mount Kilauea. The planet Jupiter's moon Io even has a volcano named in honor of Pele. This volcano is so active its glow can be detected from thousands of miles away. Pele is unique because her mythology is still in the creation process today. She has been spoken of and credited with volcanic eruptions in a religious context as late as 1907 in a formal manner.

The red Lehua flower, sacred to Pele, is used in a potion to help reduce the pain of childbirth.

Pele embodies sexual freedom; indeed, she embraces it. She is strong and temper driven. She knows who she is, and even though she may appear to be a brat at times, everything she does creates life, at the same time that she destroys it. Pele is about will. Pele is about full circle. She is raw power. She teaches us about bravery and perseverance. We can learn from Pele to be at peace with anger because good things can come from it if it is handled correctly. She shows how sometimes destruction must be used to make way for new growth.

Working with Pele in Anger Magic is natural. Always use caution, however, as she is explosive. Pele is passionate and lustful and can cause your mind to stray from its intent. She lives in the moment, and the counterpoint to control that factor is time. We must not rush when working with her.

She works best for us in the building stage and can certainly add power and oomph. Lava rock holds a natural connection to Pele and we can use it to add her energy to ours. We can use natural glass to do the same thing.

You may also align yourself with Pele using bits of hair, but you must first prepare yourself well. Connecting yourself to Pele through your hair is a long-term commitment and should not be taken lightly. Pele's priestesses were only allowed to trim their hair by the crater's edge throwing the remains down to her. Brown hair was most favored and thought to be most sacred to her. When a volcano erupts, it sends lava flying through the air where it separates into very fine individual strands of glass commonly called Pele's hair. Her priestesses believed that since Pele shared her hair, they should share theirs in return.

Modern-day renditions of the goddess Pele show her eyes alight with a fiery rage, indicative of her ability to cleanse and purify. A small working altar dedicated to her can be effective for cleansing rocks, crystals, or other small items. When calling upon her to cleanse, it is proper that we gift her with an honoring—such as burning a special incense—and ask her to "cast her cleansing sight" upon the items.

It is easy to make a volcano candle to represent Pele. It should be triple dipped—first in orange, then in red, and finally in brown—to produce an effect similar to lava when it is burned. Alternatively, you may use yellow and red wax for the core colors and black as the outer color.

Pele can help you to explode through your barriers, but she allows no room for self-martyrdom. Do not try to portray yourself as a victim; she has no patience with those who lack strength. Honesty is crucial when dealing with her or you may invoke her wrath.

The pleasure-loving Pele can be wonderful to work with during sex magic. Lustful and wanton, she can bring out your wild side.

Correspondences

Color: red, orange, black
Flora: tropical flowers and fruits
Stones: fire opal, lava rock, natural glass, amber

18. Lilith

According to Hebrew mythology, Lilith was the first female as well as the original feminist. She represents all that is wild and free within us. She embodies seduction, beauty, and defiance. She stands for the rights of women to enjoy sexual relations, and their rights to refuse any sexual relations not to their liking. A wild, raven-haired beauty, Lilith was demonized when she left Adam. Likewise, Lilith stands for something more prolific, tit-for-tat.

The best-known legend says that Lilith was created at the same time as Adam, to be his helper. She had been created from dust—the same as he—with the exception that the dust used to create Lilith was impure. When Adam attempted to mate with her he demanded a missionary position and Lilith refused to lie passive beneath him, saying, "We were created equal, and so will make love in equal positions." Adam replied that he was created in God's image and would never stoop to being only her equal. Furious, Lilith went to God and lulled him into revealing his sacred name to her. Lilith recited it and gained the power to fly away from Adam forever. She made a home in a cave, on the shores of the Red Sea and dwells there still today. She accepted demons as her lovers and birthed thousands of demons in a short time.

Adam went to God and requested Lilith be forced to return to him. God agreed and sent three angels to bring Lilith back. The angels told Lilith that if she refused God's order to return to Adam, each day one hundred of her children would be killed until she changed her mind. Lilith said she would rather lose one hundred children each day than return submissive. As the angels carried out the threat, she swore to attack the children of Adam—

and their mothers—during childbirth. She stated all newborns were in danger unless they had the protection of the three-enforcer angels displayed where she could see it. She also vowed to attack men in their sleep, stealing their seed, so that she could birth more demon children to replace those killed.

In the opera *Lilith* by Deborah Drattell and David Steven Cohen, a seer appears and says to Eve that she and Lilith are one soul, broken. That she must look inside herself and find her "dark twin" and allow herself to fall into the seduction that is Lilith. He goes on to say that doing so is the only way Eve and Lilith will find peace; as one. The thought is that Eve is flesh without shadow and Lilith is shadow without flesh.

Lilith was known to the Sumerians as the "hand of Innana." She had over forty other names, too, most of them variations of or containing the prefix *lil*—the Sumerian word for wind. She is sometimes called the Northerner: Jeremiah 1:14 says, "Out of the North, the evil breaks forth." Lilitu, or the "night hag" is another Sumerian name for Lilith. She is also known as the Black Moon and the Howling One.

Lilith is sometimes said to be the first vampire, a succubus and demoness. Sixth-century Persians assigned Lilith goddess status; she was known as the wife of Death. One school of thought says Lilith is the true mother of the biblical Cain. Accordingly, when he slew his brother Abel and was driven from the garden, it is with Lilith that he took refuge. Together they created the vampire race.

Other legends say that Lilith—upon witnessing the deaths of so many of her children—went insane. In her madness, she lost sight of proportion. When attacking human children, Lilith was said to tickle them first, and once they laughed, she would strangle them. According to one old wives' tale, tapping a laughing child on the nose would banish Lilith and keep the child safe.

There is much speculation about the origin of Lilith. Some say that the earliest text to mention her is *The Alphabets of Ben-Sira,* which dates to somewhere between the eighth and the tenth centuries. However, a prayer to Lilith appears on a tablet from Ur said to be four thousand years old. She is mentioned in the Tale of Innana and the Epic of Gilgamesh, both dating back three thousand years, and depictions of her decorate terra-cotta tablets from this time period. She is represented as a half bird–half woman with sensuous curves and claws for feet. Owls and lions stand beside her. She is crowned and has wings. She has been described as a beautiful black-haired woman with ample breasts and a lower body made of fire. Yet another description says that Lilith always wears a robe to hide her legs, which are covered in coarse black hair.

Still another legend says Lilith was born a spiritual birth—androgynously. God came forth and "sawed" Lilith from Samael's left side.

Lilith is a triple demoness—a maiden, mother, and crone version—all retaining Samael as consort. In fact, the three Liliths war within themselves.

What the Lilith myths teach us: Lilith was not afraid to fight for what she wanted, including expressing her sexuality and free will. The degree of losses she was willing to take may seem stunning, but she knew her own mind and goals and did not shy away from them. Lilith can teach us determination in the face of opposition. Lilith was a "woman scorned," and she took revenge beyond any boundaries that we would accept today. Examining these myths can help us to realize the importance of voicing our anger while tempering it with reason and rationale. Lilith helps us realize that equality is necessary for balance.

The opera mentioned shows us that acceptance of one's dark side is a priority if we hope for inner peace to be obtained.

Correspondences: Mirrors are the doorways into the world of Lilith. She is said to make a home in them. Scrying for Lilith is done by staring into your reflection's eyes. Lilith represents secrets and hidden wisdom, as she knew the sacred name of God. Lilith is the patroness of Witches. Lilith uses dreams and thoughts to make her presence known. She is raw power in the night, gaining the most strength from the waning moon. Lilith rules waste places and the desert.

Element: Air

Lunar phase: dark/waning moon; for sex magic use
the new moon.

Planet: Saturn

Floral: the lily, red roses

Stone: carnelian

Colors: red, black

Oil: patchouli

Animals: snakes, jackals, black dogs, wolves, pelicans,
wildcats, lions, owls

Tree: apple, willow

Purposes: beauty, wisdom, secrets, creativity, natural, sexual,
strength, desire, pleasure, renewal, equality,
independence. Lilith has a special affinity to red wine,
blood, and sexual fluids.

Day: Friday

Special day: Lilith is thought by some to have left the
Garden of Eden on October 24.

If you wish to work with Lilith, be warned, she is a powerful presence and you would do well to respect her. Although she will respect your strength, if you are all take and no give, there will be a price to pay. Never attempt to grovel with Lilith, she despises weakness. Working with Lilith must be approached from an equal—never a worshipful—standpoint.

On a more adult note, Lilith is extremely powerful during sex magic. While utilizing sex magic techniques, there is a strong possibility of straying from the intent. If your intent does stray while

Lilith is around, you could be in for major trouble. Do not attempt sex magic while invoking Lilith until you are positive you can perform it correctly. On the other hand, you may have someone ready to step in, if needed, to regain control.

Lilith can be helpful with sexual confidence or anxiety problems. She is *not* useful in fertility rituals and spells, however, because of the threat she represents to children. When invoking Lilith, it is better to use sex for the sake of only sex, and not procreation.

Calling on Lilith for Anger Magic is best suited to energy that has a righteous quality (for example, a situation where someone is stealing credit for work that is yours, or a cheating spouse). In these cases, Lilith can be used to pump yourself back up to a level of healthy confidence and give you the courage to stand up for yourself.

Caution is advised; Lilith does not like limitations and has no understanding of temperance. What you work for could possibly be magnified thousands of times over. For that reason it is not a good idea to approach Lilith for justice work.

Because Lilith is thought to strangle children, it is advisable to set your circle casting with a fail-safe protecting you—and all of your family—with the element of Air. Lilith needs air as she is without flesh. She flies from place to place via mental process—which again falls under the element of Air—and air itself.

Since air is vital to Lilith, it will be your strongest protection. Be careful that your wording does not make her feel threatened. Say something such as "I call the element of Air to maintain the integrity of this working with no possibility of it going astray."

Lilith is all about equality, but she is not about balance. As she has no recognition of proportion and limitations, the best magical use for her is in destruction of negative habits or traits.

If you decide to call Lilith, prepare yourself beforehand for a burst of primal fear when she arrives. You should feel it like lightning through your veins, and a sexual energy will follow closely on its heels. Keep control of your breath during this. To work with Lilith properly I recommend utilizing the Red Sea Meditation—in chapter 14 of this book—at least twice a week, for one month. It is much easier to meet Lilith gradually and become accustomed to her prior to magical work. That way her presence will not come as such a shock to the senses. You may tape-record the meditation in your voice and play it back when you are ready to meditate. Make sure you are recording your dreams in a journal throughout your Lilith meetings; she communicates primarily through them.

You may make offerings to Lilith, but I do not advise it on a regular basis. Lilith is very much a tit-for-tat entity and if you are not asking for something specific when you give her a gift, you are leaving yourself wide open to be gifted with what *she wants* to give you—she may decide to "free" you from something you have no desire to be free of.

19. Medea

The story of Medea is quite a paradox. She was once a loving mother, devoted daughter, sister, and wife; yet Medea did not shy away from murdering those in her beloved family—and she did it all for the sake of love.

Medea was and is known as the Queen of the Witches. She was a devotee of the dark goddess Hecate, and she had been taught to perform magic by her aunt Circe.

The story of Medea begins before her birth. She was the granddaughter of Helios; the sun god. Her father was King Aeetes of Colchis, the owner of the prized Golden Fleece, sought by Jason and the Argonauts. The king was of course reluctant to part with it, and he set a series of impossible tasks that must be performed before anyone else would be entitled to it.

When Medea saw Jason she fell immediately in love with him and agreed to use her magic to help him obtain the Golden Fleece, in exchange for his promise to marry her.

Upon Jason's successful completion of the tasks, the king did not keep his side of the bargain and refused to give Jason the Golden Fleece. Medea used her magic yet again and charmed the dragon that the king had charged with guarding the fleece into falling asleep. She and Jason then snatched the fleece and fled to Jason's ship, the *Argo*, with her brother Absyrtis in tow.

The king pursued them, and in an attempt to slow the pursuit, Medea killed her brother, cut his body into pieces, and scattered the parts behind the ship. The king stopped and collected the pieces of his son's body in order to give him a proper burial, which enabled Medea and Jason to escape.

Once the *Argo* returned to Jason's home country safely, Medea used her magical powers to make Jason's father, Aeson, young again by cutting his throat and restoring his body by use of a magic potion in his blood. King Pelias, who had usurped Aeson's throne in Jason's absence, was offered the same treatment. Only this time, it was a trick. Medea had convinced Pelias's daughters to cut his throat and then refused to give him the restoring potion. As a result of the king's demise, Jason and Medea had to flee to Corinth.

While there, Medea bore Jason two children and shared a happy life with him for ten years. When Jason chose to take a second wife, the daughter of King Creon, ruler of Corinth, Medea was heartbroken. She told Jason that he might well rue the day of his second marriage. The king heard of Medea's words and took them as a threat to his daughter's safety. In order to protect his daughter the king told Medea that she and her children must leave the country. A woman alone with two children and nowhere to live had no resources. Jason offered her a small crumb of pride and told her his friends would allow her and the children to live with them. Medea grew furious and decided instead to take revenge.

She sent the new bride a poisoned robe and as soon as the young princess placed it on her body, her skin burst into flame. King Creon reached out to embrace his dying child and, as a result, he was fatally poisoned.

Upon returning home and finding the dead bodies of his father-in-law and second wife, Jason—in a fury—raced to Medea's side, intent on punishing her. He found her boarding a chariot led by two winged dragons, which belonged to Helios, and saw that she was carrying the dead bodies of their two children in her arms. She had murdered her own children in order to cause Jason even more pain.

There is an alternative ending to the myth of Medea, which states that she took her children and ran to the temple of Hera for safety. The villagers, who were out for blood, found them hiding there and began throwing stones while she and the children ran to board her grandfather's chariot. The villagers, not caring that the children were innocent of any crime, stoned them to death. Medea barely escaped with her life and was falsely branded a child murderer.

What we learn from Medea: Vengeance and justice are two entirely different entities. No other tale shows this more clearly. The loss that Medea faced—and the determination to take something away from the one responsible for hurting her—only hurt her more in the end. And I believe there is much more to be considered.

As Medea was a Sorceress and a Witch, she knew certain eternal truths. As she was a devotee of Hecate, she may have thought that by killing her children she could take them away from Jason and entrust them instead to her matron goddess. She did, after all, rule the Underworld, so who better to charge with the care of her children? To Medea it would have been a holy ritual and not exactly self-sacrifice. In her mind, it might have been the kindest thing to do and done out of a great love.

Viewing it from that perspective, her family was only one small step away from her at any given time. The step of bodily death, which she could make at any moment she chose to. Therefore, one could say that vengeance or justice is all in one's perception.

Am I saying it was okay for Medea to kill her children? Of course not! I am saying in order to truly understand revenge, you must first recognize it and it is not always what it may appear to be. Motivation and intent are prime factors.

I suspect Medea's motivation was twofold. Revenge on Jason, and knowing her children were taken care of. It appears that Medea acted out of anger only, but she tempered it with the only kindness available at her disposal. The kindness of performing the children's murders herself. Parts of this myth have the nurse saying she believes Medea has turned cold toward the children. In order to relate the coldness to the murders and still see the kindness, ask yourself, What is the kindest thing you can do with something you have come to despise and love at the same time? It would be a heart-breaking choice, to be sure. Sometimes love can be even more destructive than rage and hate.

Medea claimed that it could never be said that she left her children behind for her foes to trample on. She felt she was protecting them. In "protecting" them that way, she shows us another aspect of herself—that of honor. If Jason had cast her aside so easily, perhaps he would also abandon their children. She decided it would not be left to him to choose.

Medea shows us how important it is to think any act of revenge through completely. What are the costs to you and others?

Jason used Medea for her magic and her willingness to aid him in seeking a throne. Once it was assured he no longer needed her, he chose another wife. Medea, who had done everything for the love of Jason, was abandoned.

To apply Medea to magical workings we need to examine her aspects within ourselves. While possibly a deity, Medea is certainly an entity with a vast occult knowledge. Getting to know her can be beneficial. Some have assigned her goddess status because of her family lineage, and to them she is known as the goddess of childbirth and nursing.

When dealing with Medea, never make a promise you cannot—or do not intend to—keep. To do so will provoke her, and you do not want the Queen of the Witches mad at you. Medea does not mind if you ask her for her knowledge, but you should always offer something in return so she will not feel used.

When calling Medea, keep in mind she is an entity—not necessarily a deity. It is a bit of a tricky situation, for Medea is prideful. Always show proper respect when speaking with her. Medea should be honored, as a hero and a woman before her time. She was the only heroine in the Greek tragedies who escaped with her life after such crimes. She went on to marry a king in another country.

To properly call her, set a small altar with a dragon symbol and three red candles. Use an herbal incense. Cast circle. Light the first candle and say, "For the oldest child lost, may this flame warm her heart." Light the second candle and say, "For the youngest child lost, may this flame warm her heart." Light the third candle and say, "For the woman and tragic mother, may this flame unite her family and bring her spirit to me." Know that you may visit with Medea while she enjoys a few moments with her children's love. Ask her what you will. When done, thank her for attending, bless her, and wish her farewell. Do the same for both children. You may put out the candles and close the circle now.

20. Hel

Hel, also known as Hell, Hela, and Helle, is the Norse goddess of death and ruler of the Underworld. She is the daughter of the trickster god Loki.

By the command of Odin, Hel was raised in Asgaard as an Aesir. Hel suspected that she was meant to fulfill a prophecy that called for such destruction that only evil could come from it. So Odin commanded that she be raised with the gods in order to prevent the prophecy from being fulfilled.

Hel was quite ugly, and the other gods in Asgaard often avoided her, which filled her with loneliness and despair. She explained to Odin how miserable she was and he granted her request for permission to leave Asgaard. Odin gave her one of the nine worlds to rule over, Niflheim, and even named it after her, calling it Helheim. In return, he asked that she care for the souls of those who had died in any way other than in battle or through violence. Thus, Hel came to be the goddess of the dead.

Hel has been spoken of in other myths as Brunnhilde or "Burning Hel." Brunnhilde was an honored Valkyrie who was much loved by Odin. If she is an aspect of Hel's it explains why Odin granted her one of the nine kingdoms to rule. Some versions of the myth have Odin casting her down to Niflheim cruelly, but if that is so why does he change the name to Helheim in her honor?

Hel settled into her kingdom, judging the souls as they arrived. With her eye of fire she could see lies and human faults. Helheim was believed to have nine levels, and she decided which level a soul would dwell in. The wicked were sent to the lowest realm, a place of torture and pain. The innocent found a peaceful land where all of their needs were met.

Hel is a destroyer, but only when it is necesary to act in this way. She will seek vengeance if the natural law of death is trifled with, as exemplified in the story of gambling Geoffrey: Odin and Loki gave Geoffrey money for bread, but he wagered it and lost it all. In retaliation, Odin sent Hel to him. Just as she appeared, Geoffrey was seating himself at a gaming table. She beckoned to Geoffrey to come outside, and he agreed but asked her to first climb a tree to fetch them some fruit to eat. Hel climbed up and could not get back down. Geoffrey left her there for nine years, during which time no one died. After Loki brought this to Odin's attention, Odin commanded Geoffrey to release Hel immediately. The second Hel was released from the tree, she claimed Geoffrey and carried him off to Helheim.

The story of Baldur gives an example of the iron grip Hel holds on those within her kingdom. Frigg was the second wife of Odin and mother to Baldur, the god of light, and his brother Hoder, the blind god of darkness. Frigg had the gift of sight, the ability to see into the future. She began to have visions that her son Baldur was to meet some kind of harm. In an effort to prevent this, Frigg traveled the Earth asking everything to avoid harming her beloved son. The other gods thought it was a joke and began to teasingly throw things at Baldur. They even shot arrows at him just for sport, but all of these projectiles missed their mark.

Loki slyly tricked Frigg into revealing that of all things on Earth she had allowed one sprig of mistletoe to escape the promise of no harm to Baldur. Loki immediately gathered some mistletoe and went back to the hall where the sport of taunting Baldur continued. The other gods knew he could not be hurt so they amused themselves with the game. Loki tricked Hoder into using an arrow with a mistletoe shaft, and when this arrow struck Baldur, Frigg's son fell dead.

Desperate with grief, Frigg asked for someone to go to Helheim and offer a ransom to Hel for the return of her son. She promised that anyone who would do so would be in her favor forever. Odin's son, Hermod, volunteered to make the long and difficult journey. When he finally reached Hel's hall, he found Baldur sitting in the place of honor. They spent the night in revelry together and with the morning light Hermod was granted his request to speak with Hel. He told Hel of how badly Baldur was missed. She would not be easily persuaded to give him back to the living, so she set a task. If every single thing in Aesir was not made to weep for the return of beloved Baldur, he would have to remain with Hel.

The gods in Asgaard wasted no time dispatching messengers to ask everything to weep for the return of Baldur. They came to a dark cave inhabited by an old woman giant named Thoekk, who refused to cry for Baldur and stated, "Let Hel keep what she has!" Hence, Baldur had to remain with Hel.

Sometime later the gods held a feast at which Loki became drunk and admitted to taking the form of Thoekk and being responsible for Baldur's continuing detention. To punish him for his deception, Loki's lips were sewn shut.

Hel's place within life was so sacred and secure that she fell under no god's rule and all were susceptible to her commands. With a wave of her hand she could bring about disease and decay. Her home was called misery. Hel had a knife named famine, a dish named hunger, and her bed was called the sickbed. Her kingdom was thought to be a realm of mists and ice, a frozen land. However, one part of her land included gardens with fruited bushes to delight infants and other innocent dead.

The journey to Hel's home, known as Nastrond (house of the dead), was thought to be quite a perilous trip. Her house stood high in the mountains, within a damp forest of fir trees known as the "Strand of Corpses." To get to the house, two rivers had to be forded. The first was the River Slith, a black sludgelike mixture of blood, poison, tears, and sewage with sharp debris floating in it.

The River Slith passed through the City of Suffering on the way to Helheim, and eventually emptied into the River Styx. The second was the River Gjall or River of Echoes. It could be crossed only by the Echoing Bridge, which was made of ice and gold and guarded by a warrior. The waters of the Gjall were treacherous with whirlpools. Bones float up to the surface from the churning effect, as travelers could be ground to pieces at the bottom of the churning river.

Just beyond the bridge lay the Iron Woods, where the fir trees changed into metal with sharp needles. It was almost impossible to pass through the extremely dense woods, without being sliced to ribbons.

Hel's city, Valgrind, lay just beyond these woods, directly between the two rivers.

Nastrond is thought to be an eternal plane; it will exist after everything else in the world has passed. To gain entry one must extinguish a light at the ninth door on the left hand side of the great hall. Once there, you can never escape. Hel holds those in her home with an iron grip.

Many have asserted that there is very little evidence to suggest that Hel was worshipped during her time, so much as she was simply accepted as a natural law. One only has to look at the names given to the cities of the lands in question to assume there was worship of Hel. Helsinki is the most notable one.

Hel has long been associated with dark magic and revenge. Thought to be a Witch goddess by ancient Germanic tribes, it was Hel that protected them in the dark. It was also Hel that led the procession of the Wild Hunt along with Odin. In this respect, she is related to the goddess Holda.

The wild hunt was thought to be a portent of death or war. If you stumbled upon it, it was said you would, at the very least, go insane. The wild hunt or "furious host" is always seen at night or dusk. It begins by hearing the baying and howling of dogs and shouts in the distance. Then a rider on a horse appears who is often in a state of decay as he is but a corpse. He leads a pack of the dead, some of whom may be the recently passed. The horses that carry assorted odd spirits breathe fire. The wild hunt was believed to have chased humans until they died, whereupon it would incorporate them into their ghastly parade.

In the feminine version of the wild hunt, led by Hel, the majority of the spirits involved were those of children. Hel gathered their innocent souls to lead them into her home of comfort. She was said to have given gifts to the children and to have been the original Yule spirit of Santa Claus.

What is her relation to Anger Magic? She reminds us that there are certain natural laws that we cannot affect, such as death. She also serves well in divination and weather magic practices. She can be a protector and a guide.

Hel, while a death personification, is seen as benevolent and strong. She faced her life alone and made herself so respected that she became a law of nature. Through her quiet strength and perseverance, we can be inspired to reach our own goals. Hel asked for what she wanted when she went to Odin wishing to leave Asgaard. In reward for her courageous question her wish was granted.

Correspondences

Lunar phase: dark/new
Colors: white, black
Animals: owls, ravens
Stones: moonstone, quartz, onyx, hematite, obsidian
Flora: jasmine, any other white flower
Herbs: holly
Tree: evergreens
Purposes: change, compassion, justice, death, reincarnation

21. Sekhmet

In the ancient Egyptian pantheon, Sekhmet is the lion-headed solar goddess of war, destruction, and retribution. She wears the solar serpent, the symbol of regeneration, over her brow. The hot desert winds of Egypt were said to be her breath, and the glare of the sun at midday was her body.

The divine trinity worshipped at Memphis included Sekhmet, her husband Ptah, the god of arts and crafts, and her son Nefertum, the healing god of flowers and perfume. Nefertum was often depicted with either a lion's head or standing on the back of a lion.

Sekhmet is one of the oldest goddesses in existence. She is present in Egyptian creation myths. She is said to have witnessed the beginning of time and is known as the vengeful daughter of Ra.

One legend that dates from about 2000 B.C. states that Sekhmet was the divine embodiment of the force created when the goddess Hathor was sent to Earth by Ra to take vengeance on men, who had ceased to worship Ra and were attempting to overthrow him, in order to take his powers for themselves.

Sekhmet slaughtered the evil men and drank their blood. She went wild from being drunk on the blood of men and continued her intoxicated rampage well beyond necessary. The gods felt that she would continue with her rampage until the human race had been extinguished if they did not stop her. In order to contain Sekhmet, the gods made a drug containing beer and pomegranate juice, disguised it as blood, and flooded a field with it. When Sekhmet came to the field, she licked up all the blood and fell asleep. Ra used the time to change her. When she awoke she found her rage had ceased.

Sekhmet was known as the eye of Ra and thought to be both the destructive aspect of the sun and the protector of the sun. She often used her power in a benevolent manner to heal the Earth of plagues and demons, even though she was known to send plagues herself. Her most significant attribute was that of appropriate action when it came to vengeance. She removed threats and punished those who went against the natural order.

The priests who worshipped Sekhmet were very advanced healers. These priests could set broken bones; had knowledge of anatomy, surgery, herbs, and vibrational tones; and healed mind, body, and spiritual ills.

Some of the healing methods of the Egyptians are used in Reiki today. Others hold close to the original tone and use the healing method of sekhem, which is the ancient Egyptian healing of the aura. It was gifted to the people by Sekhmet herself.

Sekhmet was feared but held in high respect. It was said that when closing out the old year and opening the new, Sekhmet had to first be appeased through a lengthy ritual; otherwise the king and the lands were in peril. There were over seven hundred statues of her in one temple at the time, and a small ritual had to be performed in front of each one in order to appease her.

Sekhmet represents a balance of the power between destruction and renewal. In her protector capacity, she maintained time and world order.

Sekhmet's name came from the word *sekhem*, the ancient Egyptian word for power. I believe this points to the existence of Sekhmet within each of us. Modern interpretations of her would have us believe she is a nurturing, mothering type of a goddess. This is a common misconception. While Sekhmet did have a son, Nefertum, she wasn't a mothering or nurturing type. Sekhmet represents many things but principally vengeance, destruction, and appropriate action.

Sekhmet is invaluable to the Anger Magic practitioner because she embodies appropriate action, clarifying for us today how sometimes the right thing may not be the easiest or most pleasant.

Sekhmet is the primal force of anger. When Ra called upon her for vengeance he was in effect calling upon the pure power of anger to be unleashed and used for destruction of his enemies. In order to stop Sekhmet's rage, he had to exert a deliberate control tactic, offering the dyed beer. We can draw a parallel of harnessing your anger and putting it to use. All while maintaining the power, within the mind, to stop the overflow of the emotion—in other words, not allowing yourself to get carried away.

Sekhmet is wonderful to deal with if applying justice to your spell work; however be prepared for it to get ugly. Not that it necessarily will, because she holds the power to transform any dark or negative situation into a positive one if she considers it to be appropriate.

To facilitate contact with Sekhmet, you might want to offer her a beer. Sekhmet loves it! It is not true that she requires a blood sacrifice: a cold brewski makes a fine and satisfactory offering.

Sekhmet can be beneficial to determination. One tip though, do not invoke her in an effort for destroying others. Work only on yourself when working with Sekhmet.

Correspondences

Color: red
Direction: south
Element: fire

Sekhmet is a solar goddess so moon phase does not matter.

22. The Erinyes

The Erinyes ("the Raging Ones") are a trio of Greek goddesses who, according to Hesiod, sprang from the freshly spilled blood of Uranus. The chthonic Greek goddess of wrath, Erinys, is a single personification of the Erinyes. They were also known as the Furies (Roman) and the Eumenides (Greek for kind-hearted) and more familiarly as the "dogs of Hades."

The Erinyes bestowed justice and sought out those who had committed crimes or wickedness. They pursued and punished the guilty who had escaped public punishment.

They dwelt deep in the heart of Hades, where they spent their time torturing the souls of wrongdoers. Nothing could change the course of their strict justice; pleading was to no avail.

Their names were Alecto ("unceasing in anger" or "endless"), Tisiphone ("avenger of murder" or "punishment"), and Megaera ("jealous one" or "jealous rage"). Described as having snakes for hair and blood dripping from their eyes, they had the bodies of old women, the heads of animals, and a set of batlike wings.

In one myth the Erinyes hounded Orestes for the sin of matricide. Unknown to the Erinyes he had killed his mother in order to avenge his father's murder at her hands. Orestes had to gain the intervention of Athena in order to get a fair trial. The Olympians decided he was not guilty, which further enraged the Erinyes. They threatened to let loose a drop of their blood upon the Earth, which would destroy all crops and the people of Athens.

According to one version of this myth, the wise Athena catered to their egos and bribed them with the offering of a sacred grotto to be devoted to their worship. This great honor placated their vengeance-seeking, and they agreed to stop hounding Orestes. Another version contends that they continued to pursue him until he sacrificed a black sheep in their honor and was therefore purified.

Orestes, grateful for the relent of his torment, gave the Erinyes the name of the Eumenides and dedicated a sanctuary to them.

Oedipus, too, was tormented by the Erinyes, in his case for the sin of patricide. Oedipus was the son of a king. His parents learned from the oracle at Delphi that their son would grow up to kill his father and marry his mother. To prevent this horror, the king and the queen understood that their son had to be destroyed; only they did not have the heart to do it themselves. They called upon a servant to leave the child in the wilds of Mount Cithaeron, where he would surely meet his demise all alone in the beast-filled wilderness. The servant took pity on the hapless baby, however, and found a kind couple to take him in.

Oedipus was raised as a happy child. One day children in the village were fighting, and one of them let it slip that Oedipus was not the "real" son of his parents. Upset, Oedipus confronted his parents, who swore he was indeed their real son.

To discover the truth Oedipus went to the oracle at Delphi and asked, "Who am I?" The oracle replied only that he was a man who would kill his father and marry his mother. Oedipus was understandably both confused and devastated.

He decided not to return home but instead to go to the city of Thebes, in order to keep his beloved parents safe from the oracle's dire prediction. He determined to stay away. As he approached a crossroads, he came upon an older man with a chariot and attendants. The man in the chariot yelled at him, struck him with his staff, and ran over his foot with the chariot wheel. Oedipus grabbed the staff and landed one fatal blow to the man's head. He fought off the attendants, leaving only one alive, who ran away.

Oedipus continued on to Thebes, where he met and fell in love with the recently widowed queen. They lived together for many years happily ruling Thebes, until one day the city was struck with a plague. King Creon appeared and told Oedipus that until the true murderer of the former king had been brought to justice, the plague would remain on the city, according to the oracle at Delphi. "How is it this has not been done?" Oedipus asked. Creon replied that there had been only one surviving witness and that witness was out of his mind from fear. He was very old now and had lived in a hut in the mountains ever since Oedipus had begun his rule. Oedipus ordered that he be found at once.

Oedipus then proceeded to place a formal curse upon the murderer of the old king, without knowing who that was. He called upon the blind prophet Teiresias, hoping to find out the truth. The prophet begged Oedipus not to ask, admonishing that it was for his own good. Angered, Oedipus ordered an answer from the prophet. Teiresias replied, "Before the sun is down you will find yourself both husband and son, father and brother."

Convinced the prophet was lying, Oedipus was soon to discover by speaking with the one remaining witness that the prophet's words were indeed true. He was wed to his mother and had killed his father at the crossroads, all without his knowledge. So he became subject to the torment of the Erinyes, who knew nothing of mercy.

According to the myth of Alcmaeon, he was driven to madness by the Erinyes because he carried out his father's order to kill his mother—in order to call a halt to a dreadful ongoing war. The Erinyes, in this capacity, relate to a guilty conscience. They would often drive their victims to suicide. They placed particular importance on familial killings.

To say that people were afraid of the Erinyes would be an understatement. Older than the Olympians, the Erinyes fell under no god's rule, but they did honor Zeus and held him in high esteem. Their function was much higher than that of any of the Olympian gods however. They were so powerful that had Zeus himself committed a transgression, the punishment would be meted out by the Erinyes. They were even said to be responsible for keeping the sun in the sky.

The Erinyes originally knew only their function as dispensers of justice. Mitigating circumstances were not considered. While their actions are of a righteous nature, they were immortal goddesses. As humans, refusing to consider all circumstances does not make us righteous, it makes us self-righteous. The Erinyes would continue their tormenting even after death. Only when remorse was shown would they relent.

The ways of the Erinyes are the opposite of what the Anger Magic practitioner's goals should be. The Erinyes saw only black and white. We must strive to see all things as gray. Mitigating circumstances should always come into play in our decisions. We may discard them, but we have to acknowledge and examine them.

Another thing we can learn from the Erinyes is strength. They fulfilled their calling no matter what. Once we reach a decision, we need the courage to follow through. The Erinyes teach keeping us to our course. They allow for no second-guessing once a choice has been made.

Calling upon the Erinyes for aid in making a justice decision is not recommended. Calling upon them for a truth search is. The Erinyes can be of great use to us in uncovering forgotten facts, blocked memories, and the events that have shaped us. The Erinyes allow us to remember them without fear. They do not like lies and will help us to burst through even the lies we tell ourselves.

A few things to note when calling the Erinyes for a truth search: If your questions concern your relationship with your parents, be prepared for the Erinyes to side with them, not you. For this reason I suggest asking for the knowledge of specific events instead of general lifetime hurts. If you ask for knowledge only relating to one event, you are not risking finding out things that you are ill prepared to deal with.

To call the Erinyes for a truth search, prepare an altar with three white candles, fresh flowers, a floral incense, three glasses of cool water, paper and a pen, matches, and a burning dish. Light the incense. Cast circle. With the pen, write your question on the paper. Begin your call with Alecto. Say, "Alecto! I ask to bear your presence, the truth I must know!" Light one of the candles. Say, "Tisiphone! I ask to bear your presence, the truth I must know!" Light another candle. Say, "Megaera! I ask to bear your presence, the truth I must know!" Light the last candle. Offer the water or wine to them by holding the glasses one at a time to the air. Say something from the heart, along the lines of, "The question on the paper before me needs a truthful answer in order to be remedied. I ask for you to remove the lies I tell myself concerning this. I am sorry for the lies I have imposed on myself. I ask to see only this truth." Set the paper on fire. You may either scry the flames or bury the ashes and wait. The truth will come to you. Maybe in a dream or vision, but it will be there. The Erinyes can also be helpful in transformations and necessary retribution.

23. Chaos and Eris

I n a time before the Earth, there was only Chaos, according to Hesiod. Chaos birthed our world into existence, one god at a time, from herself. Over the course of our evolution, we have tried to establish an orderly society. However, being birthed from Chaos, this can never be under our complete control. To paraphrase Nietzsche, we must hold chaos within—if we hope to birth a dancing star.

Chaos was the endless void that turned herself inside out to create us. Because she did, she is the mother of science and philosophy, a theory still very relevant today.

Ovid described Chaos as a "rough unordered mass of things." The Egyptians saw her as the ocean. The Norse saw her as a mist. The Chinese saw her as a cosmic egg. Nevertheless, all thought that life sprang from Chaos; she was pivotal to the creation of our world.

According to Roman mythology, after the elements separated Chaos took the form of the great two-faced male god, Janus, the supreme the god of gods. His two faces represented the confusion that lingered from Chaos, and the month of January is named in his honor.

In Greek myths Chaos does not have a personality, as such. To find a persona that fits Chaos, many look to the Greek goddess Eris (known by the Romans as Discordia), the goddess of discord and strife. She was the constant companion to Ares, the Greek god of war. Some think she was his twin and the daughter of Zeus and Hera. Others assert her to be the child of Nyx. Eris was hatred personified. She delighted in bloodshed and suffering.

Because of her disagreeable nature, she was the only god not invited to the wedding of Peleus and Thetis. She went anyway and was refused admittance. This so enraged her that she took a golden apple and inscribed the words, "To the fairest" on it and threw it in among the guests. Hera, Athena, and Aphrodite immediately each laid claim to the prize. They began to argue and asked for Zeus to decide who deserved the apple and the title. Zeus refused to do so and sent them instead to Paris, a local shepherd who was well known for being a keen judge of beauty.

When the three goddesses came upon Paris, each one tried to bribe him to pick her. Aphrodite promised him the most beautiful woman in the world as his bride, and Paris succumbed to her persuasion and chose her as fairest.

Helen of Troy was well known for being the most beautiful woman on Earth, and Paris set off to Sparta to fetch her. When he got there he found that she was already married—and to a king at that. Since he considered her to be his, per Aphrodite's promise, he kidnapped her and took her back to Troy. The king retaliated by beginning the Trojan War in order to get Helen back—all this at the behest of Eris and all because of spite.

When Pandora opened the box and released all of the ills into the world, they were said to be the offspring of Eris. She was held to have given birth to strife, toils, forgetfulness, starvation, pain, fighting, lies, disputes, ruin, murder, sorrow, quarrels, and lawlessness. To say she was a goddess despised is probably true, but she was nevertheless respected and feared. Even the Olympians were afraid of her vengeful wrath.

When Eris roamed the battlefields she would bring along the two attendants of Ares—Panic and Dread—as she would relish the fighting and suffering. She was known to shout gleefully when the Earth became soaked in the blood of warriors.

Eris fosters hatred among men, turning disagreement into destruction and bloodshed.

However, it is also the essence of Eris to inspire men to reach higher to achieve their goals. Strangely she accomplishes this through jealousy. It is up to each person to decide how to respond to jealousy. We can allow it to destroy us or we can see it manifest as healthy competition.

In modern goddess books, I often find the myths of Eris watered down and turned into some sort of shelter for the worshipper. Eris is not a shelter; she is the goddess of confusion. Her goal is to create discord and harm. Her wishes are that the suffering inflicted by confusion escalate unto death, her greatest joy. The principles of Anger Magic work directly against Eris in many ways and yet through her. Do not try to whitewash her into being a loving type of goddess. We have to see her as she really is in order to learn from her.

Anger Magic practitioners can learn many things from Eris's example. We can learn to thoroughly check our actions. We can learn to examine things over and over if need be, to rid ourselves of confusion. We also gain from the inspiration of destruction. Since Eris is credited with inciting destruction within us, she is useful to us in a very pertinent way.

It is the nature of Chaos to contradict. It is the nature of Eris to constantly inspire contradiction in our thoughts in an attempt to confuse us. Contradicting ourselves leads us to question all that we know. However, it also helps us gain clarity by questioning every aspect of a situation. Eris inspires us to continuously evolve and become better.

Because of the free-thinking ethical system required for Anger Magic we can use Chaos and Eris to our advantage. However, I do not suggest attempting any sort of communication from a worshipful standpoint. It is better in the case of these two goddesses that we recognize them inside ourselves.

24. Nemesis

Nemesis was the Greek goddess of retribution, justice, and law; she punished those responsible for evil deeds and excessive misbehaviors of any sort.

According to Hesiod, the mother of this "lower Olympian" was Nyx, and her father was Erebus. Some sources say her father was either Oceanus or Zeus.

One function served by Nemesis was holding her free-hearted partner, Tyche (good fortune) in check. If Tyche smiled upon you and sent undeserved blessings your way, Nemesis would counteract her by sending misfortune. Arrogance and insolence fueled her fire, as did any unsociable act. Known as the right hand of Zeus, Nemesis was often depicted with a finger to her lips as if saying "Silence!"

Polycrates, the tyrant of Samos, was one upon whom extreme and undeserved good fortune had been bestowed. In an effort to placate Nemesis in advance, he threw his most prized possession, a priceless ring, into the sea. A fish swallowed it and a fisherman later returned the ring to Polycrates, indicating that Nemesis had refused the offering. Shortly thereafter, Polycrates was killed and his corpse was crucified.

Nemesis was thought to be as beautiful as the goddess Aphrodite. In one legend, she was overcome by Zeus himself, while he was disguised as a swan. The story goes that Aphrodite made Zeus fall in love with the beautiful Nemesis. Nemesis tried to evade Zeus by changing herself into a fish, then later on into a goose. Zeus took the form of a swan and Aphrodite took the form of an eagle and chased him. Nemesis rescued the poor swan and fell asleep with him in her arms.

Zeus, not one to waste an opportunity, ravished her in her sleep and then flew away. A few months later Nemesis laid a beautiful blue-and-silver egg and left it in the forest. Hermes found the egg and gave it to Leda. When the egg hatched—out popped Helen of Troy, the most beautiful woman in the world. Leda raised her as her own, but her true parents were Zeus and Nemesis.

In the early Greek myths, Nemesis was portrayed with beautiful wings and shining white clothing. In the later myths, she is described as monstrous and cruel. It was her function to uphold balance in the universe by bringing about justice. She comes off cruel at times; however her function is much higher than that of human perceived cruelty or wrath. Her most important personification is that of righteous indignation.

An example of this can be found in the legend of Narcissus, the son of the nymph Leiriope and the river god Cephissus. His parents consulted the famed seeker Theiresias and asked if their son would be blessed with a long life. Theiresias replied, "He will have a long life; as long as he never knows himself."

Narcissus was so beautiful that anyone who saw him would fall in love with him. By the age of sixteen, he had callously broken many hearts and rejected many suitors because his pride in his own beauty was so great.

One of his hopeful suitors was the young wood nymph Echo, who could only speak what she had last heard. Therefore, when Narcissus called to her all she could do was repeat his last words back to him. Narcissus cruelly shoved her away and told her, "I will never lie with you!"

Echo was beside herself in her heartbreak and she spent the rest of her life in lonely places pining away for her beloved Narcissus. Before she died Echo appealed to Nemesis for help and the goddess devised a unique retribution.

When Narcissus came to a spring, bent down to get a drink of water, and caught sight of his beautiful image, he instantly fell in love. Hour after hour, he sat gazing at himself, until it finally dawned on him that he was seeing his own reflection. When he tried to kiss himself he drowned.

Another version of the myth says that the suitor was not Echo, but instead a young man named Ameinius. When Narcissus rejected him, Ameinius was so heartbroken that he committed suicide. Nemesis stepped in to see balance restored by punishing Narcissus with death as well. In this version, Narcissus dies from plunging his dagger into his heart. Nemesis was not angry, she was simply right.

Nemesis does not like superiority complexes or attempting to judge yourself better than others. As it was her duty to balance the callous cruelty of Narcissus she had him fall in love with himself so that he would know the heartbreak of loving what he could not have. Such was divine justice.

Nemesis is extremely useful to Anger Magic. In the personification of righteous indignation, she allows us a freedom to accept our own judgments. As long as we are fair to all, we are following her example.

Her name is used today to represent one's downfall, problem area, or enemy. However, when taking the myths into account we can see that she is far from an enemy but is simply the essence of what is right.

Correspondences

Lunar phase: waxing
Tree: ash
Colors: indigo blue, silver, white
Purposes: legal matters, justice, retribution, balance
Symbol: scales
Special day: August 23 was her feast day
Animals: griffins, fish, geese

25. Correspondences

The correspondences in Anger Magic run the gamut of the usual herbs, stones, colors, and the like. However, it also features correspondences that are unique in their functions as anger facilitators or conductors. You may find the following list a bit odd and you may have your own unique correspondences to add to it. Correspondences appropriate for specific deities have been listed within the chapters about each deity.

A note of warning: Many of the herbs listed in this chapter are poisonous, so take extreme care if you attempt to use them. I do not recommend using them in any fashion; they are listed here as reference only. Many of the herbs emit a poisonous smoke when burned. (*Never* burn them indoors and be very careful outdoors!) Never ingest them. The poisonous herbs are indicated by an asterisk (*) beside their name; you can use tobacco as a substitute for any of them; in fact, I recommend that you do. Also, take care when working with the flammables and explosives. Follow basic safety rules at all times.

Stones

Amethyst: Amethyst is good for clarity and intuition. It also bolsters courage. Amethyst blocks anger and works well as a barrier.

Apache's tears: These are good for maintaining control when carried or worn.

Black obsidian: This stone inspires anger in some. Ringing a candle with an obsidian stone at each cardinal point can set up aggressive energies to be directed where you like. Select the appropriate candle color to correspond with your intent. You may also use a representation of something you wish to destroy instead of a candle.

Bloodstone: Bloodstone has a strong protective vibration. It also helps hold your magic to its intent. It can be used to boost aggressiveness and also to relieve stress.

Carnelian: Carnelian was worn in ancient Egypt by those wishing to relieve themselves of anger or hatred. It boosts courage.

Citrine: Citrine is cleansing and absorbing. Place it on chakra points to soak up hidden anger.

Flint: Flint is a good stone for protection against fairies. If you set a boundary that you need to keep free from other entities, setting flint about the cardinal points of it can maintain the purity.

Garnet: A garnet is particularly useful to the Anger Magic practitioner as it can bring hidden anger to the surface. It will also radiate that same anger as a force field of protection around you.

Hematite: This stone is particularly good for grounding and use in chakra absorption. Place it on the affected chakra and allow it to absorb any trapped energy.

Jet: Jet makes a wonderful storage facility for anger.

Lava rock: Lava rock holds natural protection and acts as a mirror for anger directed at you. It reflects it back to the sender.

Lepidolite: Relieves anger, tension, and stress. This stone is wonderful for storing anger while awaiting transformation. It often transforms the energy for you.

Rose quartz: Rose quartz is good for soothing angry feelings between loved ones.

Ruby: This energizing stone has a particularly good function in Anger Magic. When in a negative place it turns darker. It can alert you to danger that you do not otherwise perceive.

Sulfur: Sulfur mimics the magical properties of anger. It is protective. It works well in banishing, cursing, and healing. Sulfur is a soft material and can be powdered for spell use.

Herbs

*Aconite: Aconite is also known as Wolf's bane. Since it is poisonous, it works well in matters of destruction. However, aconite can be used for much more than that. It is protective in nature and if used as a shield against the energy of others it is unparalleled. Aconite may be used in spells or rituals to transform the anger of others.

Adam and Eve root: To rid yourself of competitors carry these with you. They can also be used to call a halt to a hurtful love situation.

Agrimony: Agrimony works as a mirror for bad vibrations.

Angelica root: The Angelica root relates to personal power. It can be used to strengthen and boost the individual. It works especially well for women.

Apple: Apples have unique characteristics. The flesh of the apple is a love representation and has long been used in love spells, but the seeds hold the ingredient to one of the most deadly poisons known to man, cyanide. Never ingest the seed. Apple seeds can be used to rid yourself of hurtful feelings after a failed love affair.

Apples, in a metaphorical sense, show that within all love lies death at the root; and that a pretty surface does not mean something is pretty at the core. Looking at the apple when you slice it in half you will notice the core holds a pentagram shape with the seeds in the center. This can be seen as a core of death with divinity wrapped around it, followed by a growth of our world on the outside. Death is at the center, and within the seeds of all beginnings lay the seeds of the end.

Asafetida: I recommend strong caution with this herb; it stinks! However, it is good for banishing whatever you've had a difficult time getting rid of.

Banana: Bananas can be used to honor Pele, or as a male phallic representation. Since banana trees die after they bear fruit, they represent the futility of material possessions. They can be eaten to build sexual energy. Burning the outer peel removes negativity.

Basil: Basil is used as a cleansing agent after Anger work. It can also be used for banishing.

Bay: Bay has a purifying vibration and can also be used to call your anger home or to correct spells that may have run a bit amok.

*Belladonna: Belladonna's use in Anger Magic stems from the plant's toxicity. In the past, it was used to encourage visions and astral projection, but for Anger Magic purposes, it is used for the destruction of blocks.

Benzoin: Benzoin is a strong clearing herb; it cleanses things and areas very well. A benzoic tincture may be used as a preservative.

Black hellebore: Black hellebore is poisonous, so it works well as a destructive herb. It may be burned, buried or crumbled.

Black mustard seeds: Scatter these about to disrupt a pattern of energy. This works especially well to keep others out of your business.

Black pepper: Black Pepper has an absorbent quality. It can be used to rid yourself of unwanted influences. The same way that black pepper produces a sneeze when you sniff it, it can have the effect of pushing anger out of the body when touched to the tongue or eaten. If you are having a hard time expelling your anger for use, try black pepper. It will absorb it and force it out.

Blackberry leaves: The leaves of a blackberry plant can be used as a mirror, to send negative vibrations away from you and back to their point of origin.

Bleeding heart: When grown indoors, bleeding heart can boost angry energy. Crushing the flowers will stimulate anger.

Calamus: Calamus is used in spellwork to gain control of or dominate a situation. It may be placed on the altar, powdered, burned or buried.

Camphor: The smell of camphor is known to dull the sexual appetite. It can be used in any case where you suspect sexual abuse. Simply allow the aroma to waft or sprinkle about.

Castor beans: Castor beans absorb bad vibrations. Castor oil has the same qualities and may be used as a substitute.

Cayenne pepper: Cayenne is an anger stimulator. It can be used in spells to increase hostility and as a building agent.

Chicory: Chicory can be carried to destroy any and all obstacles. The root may be used in spells for cursing.

Cinnamon: Cinnamon can be used in spells to inspire creative notions.

Cinquefoil: Cinquefoil is also known as five-finger grass. It is used in spellwork for breaking negative cycles and in compelling others to grant you a favor.

Clove: Clove can be used in spells to stop the actions of another. It works well when dealing in matters of intervention or in works designed to cancel out negative cycles. Clove also can be used in spells to instill passion.

Cypress: The cypress is a death herb. It can be used in spellwork to put a swift end to something, or to transform it into something else entirely.

Dill: Dill, especially the seeds, can be sprinkled about to dispel negative vibrations. It is said that carrying it can make you irresistible.

Dragon's blood: Dragon's blood is used in spells as a power boost or enhancer. Smelling it can be good for calling your anger out in its full capacity.

Eucalyptus: Eucalyptus has the ability to cast off evil or negative vibrations. It is a healing plant.

Fern: Burn a small piece of fern when you need to conjure a storm of anger within. Fern also can guide you to deep wells of stored anger if you meditate while burning it. Burning fern has the reputation of bringing about rain.

Garlic: Garlic can be used to loosen magical vibrations. Eating it causes bad spirits to leave the area and burning it can help clear storms. Garlic is also absorbent, so it works well as a storage facility.

Ginger: Ginger is a hot herb. It is good in matters of destruction and also boosts power. It has been known to incite anger in some.

Heather: Heather is a deterrent to violence; carry a bit with you to avoid losing your self-control. If you choose to burn heather for the same reason, be aware that it has a reputation for conjuring ghosts when burned.

*Hemlock: The juice of hemlock can be used to strengthen the power of an athame, used to cut the veil between the worlds. It can also add strength to clearing a fog from the memory in the same manner. Dip the athame in the hemlock juice, and visualize it cutting through the damaged memory curtain.

Honeysuckle: Honeysuckle is a powerful banishing plant. It is also protective.

Hyacinth: Hyacinth can be used in spellwork to keep others out of your business.

Lemon: Lemon can be used as a poppet. It can also be used to "sour" a situation as a cursing agent. Lemon juice is purifying and cleansing as well. It works well when used to sour your taste for a bad habit.

Loosestrife: This herb is said to end arguments and break negative patterns.

Mallow: Mallow can be used in spells to make another think of you.

Mandrake: Mandrake is used as an absorbent in Anger Magic. To stimulate the absorbent properties of mandrake root you will need to activate it by soaking it in water for three days or so (save the water for blessing and protection use). Once activated, you can place a small piece of mandrake in the area where you wish to absorb the vibrations. You may also use mandrake as a storage facility.

Marjoram: Marjoram is protective. It will guard not only the practitioner, but also keep harm away from the practitioner's family.

Masterwort: Masterwort boosts self-control.

Milk thistle: If you wear milk thistle around your neck, your aggressiveness may increase to the point of starting fights.

Mugwort: Mugwort has many powers; the one we will utilize it for the most in Anger Magic is the power of prevention. Mugwort inside the home can keep anger or hostile feelings out. It makes a good substitute for belladonna. It also works well as a cleansing agent after Anger work.

Myrrh: Myrrh is beneficial when used in contemplating justice matters or matters of the heart. It also works as a power boost to any other ingredient you may combine it with.

Nettle: Nettle has the ability to "eat" things. It does not destroy the thing per se, but can easily be fed problems.

Onion: The onion works well as an absorbent of vibrations and to "throw away your tears." It makes an excellent purge.

Orris root: The orris root enhances feelings of calm and can soothe troubled areas.

Parsley: Parsley had a reputation among the ancient Greeks as a death herb. If you wish to end something permanently, parsley can help. By cutting parsley, you may cut ties with someone.

Passionflower: Passionflower calms troubles and attracts good vibrations.

Patchouli: Patchouli can be used to banish as well as to bind. It works as a substitute for graveyard dirt as it has the rich aroma of earth. Patchouli works well as a grounding agent, and it can be used to instill passion.

Pennyroyal: Pennyroyal helps to ease stress within marital situations.

Pine: Pine is a cleansing and protective herb.

Pistachio: The pistachio nut can be used to see the whole of a situation and put an end to it.

Pomegranate: The juice of a pomegranate can be used as a substitute for blood.

Poppy: Poppy can be used to put a problem to sleep. The seeds work well to create confusion.

Potato: The potato is commonly used as a poppet. Hollowed out, it makes a good container for purging angry energy.

Primrose: Primrose can alleviate a child's resentment and anger at a parental figure.

Rose: Rose can both instill and calm passions.

Rosemary: Rosemary can be used for protection, cleansing, and transformation of the emotions. To increase feelings of anger, tie rosemary to your left arm; to dispel anger, tie rosemary to your right arm.

Rue: Rue clears the mind and allows you to see things without emotions clouding your view.

Sage: Sage is used for cleansing before and after anger work.

St. John's wort: St. John's wort is known to get the truth from others. If you suspect you are being lied to, place it in the mouth of a poppet to learn the truth.

Sesame: Sesame opens the doors to the mind. If you are having trouble with the meditations or locating your anger stems, sesame can help.

Slippery elm: Slippery elm can bind another person's tongue.

Snapdragon: The flower of the snapdragon can be held in the hand when in danger of losing your temper. This works well as an aid when waiting out a situation.

Summer savory: This herb improves the mental processes.

Thyme: Thyme works well under the pillow at night to keep nightmares away.

Tobacco: Tobacco can be used in place of any of the poisonous herbs, either in spellwork or as offerings. Watch the smoke for apparitions; they sometimes appear when you burn tobacco.

Valerian root: Valerian root has enjoyed its reputation as "nature's valium" for a long time now. It can be a good aid for relaxation. It serves a dual purpose, as it can also be used for destruction.

Venus flytrap: The Venus flytrap plant can be grown for the sole purpose of feeding it problems. It is also very protective of the environment around it.

Vervain: The juice of the vervain plant can be used to dull the sexual appetite. You can use it in spellwork whenever you suspect sexual abuse.

Witch hazel: Witch hazel cools passions and keeps temper tantrums at bay.

*Wormwood: Wormwood can be used for conjuring spirits, but more important, it can work as a magnet. When added to other spell ingredients, wormwood increases the power. Wormwood can be used for cursing. The smoke from wormwood is poisonous when burned.

Yarrow: Yarrow conquers fears and cleanses all vibrations to the neutral point. An infusion of yarrow can be used to clear the energy contained in storage stones. Yarrow has the ability to transform anger back to raw energy.

*Yew: Yew is poisonous and works well as a destructive herb. It can end problems.

Yucca: The yucca plant works as a transformer for anger. Ringing a storage facility with yucca ensures that the vibrations transform to raw energy.

Colors

Anger Magic color correspondences are unique; they depend on the *shade* as much as the primary color. Darker shades absorb vibrations whereas lighter shades reflect them. Therefore, the color correspondences fall into color families. You select the primary color according to intent, and go either darker or lighter as needed. Within each color family, the shades can run into the hundreds.

For example, if you wished to perform a spell for soaking up extra courage, you would choose a dark shade from the red family. If you were working a spell for deflecting unwanted sexual advances, you would choose a lighter shade of red.

Black: Black is always absorbent. It can be used for cursing, binding, banishing, protection, and return-to-sender tactics. If the intent is to absorb, black can substitute for any other color.

Blue: The color blue represents truth, wisdom, protection, harmony, patience, and peace. Within the blue family, there are specific uses for indigo and darker gray-blue shades. Indigo is known as a neutralizer, a karma balancer, and an aid in meditation. The darker gray-blue shades are used to create confusion.

Brown: Brown denotes stability, influence, favors, concentration, and balance.

Gray: Use gray for legal matters, transformations, and Otherworld communications.

Green: Use green for fertility, abundance, prosperity, renewal, beginnings, and healing. Within the green family, there is a specific use for the lighter yellow-green shades: deflecting jealousy.

Orange: Use orange to exhibit joy, ambition, flexibility, and control.

Purple: The color purple signifies spirituality, divination, honor, and idealism.

Red: Red denotes energy, passion, strength, sexual prowess, courage, willpower, and action. Within the red family, we find specific uses for magenta and pink. Magenta is known to influence the timing of a spell. Due to its high vibrational frequency, it brings fast results. Pink is used for matters of love, affection, beauty, and romance.

White: White is always reflective. It can be used in matters of protection, truth, peace, purity, and higher power. White can substitute for any other color as long as the intent is to reflect.

Yellow: Yellow represents creativity, happiness, laughter, intellect, and mental powers.

Specialty Items

Alcohol: Alcohol is a cleansing agent, flammable and yet cold on the skin. It is neutral and can be used in spellwork for almost anything. Simply charge it with intent or herbs.

Animal hair: Especially powerful are the hairs from black animals. Using the hair will add needed energy if, at any time, your own has dwindled.

Ash wood: The wood of the ash tree works well as an absorbent material. It makes an excellent storage facility.

Blood: Blood in magic has extreme power. It can be used for any sort of magic, however is not necessary. Bringing out blood is the equivalent to bringing out the big guns.

Charcoal: The function of charcoal in Anger Magic is unique. Commonly, Witches use charcoal to burn things upon, such as herbs or incense. Charcoal contains the fire within itself so it can be used alone for Anger Magic. It serves the same function as a candle, but leaves you the option of grinding it together with other spell ingredients to create a base for future Fire Magic. In addition, charcoal is absorbing. You can make use of this function by holding it and transferring your own vibrations into it, or allow it to soak up negativity in whole rooms. It can draw anger away from you and into itself. Charcoal is invaluable to the Anger Magic practitioner. It can be used metaphorically and physically in control exercises and meditations because of its long-burning effect.

Eggshells: For use in Anger Magic the eggshells should be whole but empty. Poke a small hole in each end and blow out the contents of the eggshell. It may now be used as a container. Eggshells are absorbent and easily crushed fine for use in magical powders.

The eggshell can be used as a symbol of our world when we wish to work for change, and it can also be of significant use for bursting through barriers.

Flammables: Potions for Anger Magic can be worked into an alcohol base, giving them flammability. Combining fire with the potion ingredients, such as lighting it in a cauldron, is added "oomph." For example, if you take an alcohol base, it relates to the element of Water. The herbs and additives relate to Earth and Air (from the aroma) and lighting it adds the element of Fire. Your actions charge the potion with spirit. Flammables are very powerful as a base for potions. Make sure to practice safety rules at all times.

Graveyard dirt: We use graveyard dirt to lay things to rest. Graveyard dirt may be used as a hexing agent. Graveyard dirt is the one exception to the powers of Earth canceling out angry vibrations. Some graveyard dirt will have angry vibrations of its own.

Gunpowder: This serves the same purpose as flammables except it is used in magical powders, rather than liquid.

Iron: Iron has the capacity to block anger. Anger cannot penetrate iron and must therefore flow around it. It is very successful as a barrier. It can block negative energies of any sort and those it cannot block, it will absorb. Sickness, for instance, can be drained from the body by wearing a piece of iron jewelry. The uses for iron in Anger Magic are many and varied. Iron projects a blinding energy force. It has a strong protective magical quality and is good for grounding. Iron can be used to block the energies of others to avoid attack. Conversely, iron is ruled by Mars, the war planet, and iron filings or rust are sometimes used in potions and powders to create hostility.

Magnets: You can use natural magnets such as lodestones or even refrigerator magnets if need be. The purpose of the magnet is to attract something to you. Oil, water, and so forth, can attain the magical property of attracting by soaking a magnet in it for thirty days.

Saltpeter: Saltpeter serves the same purpose as gunpowder.

Sand: Sand is special as it is of the Earth but has the capacity to contain angry energy rather than cancel it out. It is the perfect storage medium.

Sweat: This works well for "linking" in sympathetic magic.

Tears: Tears serve the same purpose as sweat. They are used for healing and cleansing as well.

Vinegar: Vinegar has a double function. Since the essence of it is pure, it can be used either to sour a situation or as a cleansing agent. While it is a liquid, vinegar has an absorbent quality. Placed in an open container in the center of a room, it will draw all negative vibrations (along with many odors) into itself.

Special Timing

Autumn and summer: The autumn season is associated with windy days. Summer is associated with the sun and heat. Anger Magic works best in these two seasons, but it works almost as well year-round. July is especially potent for Anger Magic, in relation to ridding yourself of negativity and beginning new and positive cycles.

Lunar eclipse: The lunar eclipse holds a special function in Anger Magic. It is an opportune time to perform spells of destruction.

Samhain: Samhain is especially powerful for Anger Magic, as it is the day when the veil between worlds is at the thinnest.

Saturdays: In Anger Magic, Saturday is the most effective day to perform banishing spells.

Storms: Storms that encompass thunder and lightning can be strong boosters for the magic. Tornados, hurricanes, and other windy storms are excellent as well. However, if a storm features a torrential downpour of rain it may have a smothering effect.

Tuesdays: Tuesday was named after the planet Mars, known as the War planet. Aggressive vibrations are said to peak on Tuesdays. Spells designed to destroy work best on Tuesdays.

IV. Putting Anger Magic to Work

Spells, Rituals, and Recipes

26. Spells

Each of the spells listed in this chapter comes from my personal Book of Shadows, and all of them work quite well. You may use them as they are, or as a starting point in creating your own spells. The main things to remember when employing Anger Magic are to always first cast a sacred circle, and to build your anger to a furious point. When you speak in a spell, allow the anger to come through in your voice. Do not be afraid of sounding overly dramatic, you are supposed to be passionate. Just let it all flow naturally.

Let's look back to the stewpot. When creating an angry spell the purpose is the stew's base, the fire to cook it on is the anger. Everything else is just seasoning.

Weight Loss

SUPPLIES:
One yellow candle
Honeysuckle oil

Cast your sacred circle. Anoint the candle with the oil in a banishing motion. Now I want you to get good and mad at your excess weight. It has cost you a lot of money, a lot of time, and a lot of heartache. Think of all the clothes you have that no longer fit you. Build it. Raise it. Call to the element of Air, "I seek thine aid! I will that you take from me fifteen (or however many) pounds, along with it take my blessings and thanks!" Dance. There is no need to be shy or self-conscious about it, just dance like a madwoman. Allow yourself to be worked into a furious pace. Think of whatever you have to think about to build your anger up to a high level. Once it has peaked, pull it in to your center and transfer it into the candle. See it as a wave of fat-dissolving energy flowing into the candle. You may feel as though it is being "torn" from you; scream as you release it if you like. When you are breathless and feel the frenzy is gone, your work is done. Light your candle. Say, "So it is done!" and close circle.

Energy Booster

SUPPLIES:

1 piece of quartz crystal

This spell can be done anywhere, anytime. When you are angry, take the crystal into your right hand and pour the anger in. See the red energy flowing into the crystal, where it promptly becomes white. Each time you are inconvenienced by anger, transfer it into this stone. When you feel it is full, bring a pot of water to boil. In it, place a dash of blessed salt and a penny. Say, "Blessed salt, through the Great Mother you do neutralize and transform the energy contained in this stone. By the boiling of the stone, it is once again pure. As Water changes to Air, the steam released from the water is now the raw energy you have recycled for me and I choose to use it for———. So Mote It Be!"

Destroy Smoking

SUPPLIES:

1 Lemon
Knife
1 black cloth bag
1 cigarette

Raise your anger level to high. At your peaking, rip the cigarette into shreds and split the lemon in half with the knife. Sprinkle the tobacco on the lemon halves. Spit at them. Tell the little brown flakes how much you hate them. See the smoke curling into your body and causing damage. Get really mad about it. Give it back. Tell the tobacco it can have all of its harm back, for your body will have none of it! Now visualize your tissues turning pink and healthy again. Close up the lemon, place it in the black bag and bury it somewhere off of your property. It is done.

Stop Gossip

SUPPLIES:
Patchouli incense
1 red candle
1 black candle
Slippery elm powder

The red candle represents the gossip; the black candle represents your power to stop it. Cast circle and set incense to smoking. Roll both candles in the slippery elm powder. Light the red candle and say out loud the rumor you wish to stop. Raise your anger to a furious point and channel it into the black candle. Say, "I now call upon my goddess to aid me in the destruction of this unfair gossip! Mother, your child is suffering and in need. I send my will and energy to do this task and know that you will destroy the hurtful words with no harm to anything else. So it must be and it is so!" Light the black candle. Allow the flame to melt the wax a bit and then drip the melted wax onto the red candle saying, "With this drop, the gossip will stop." Repeat until there is a good coating of black on the red candle. Put out the black candle. Close circle and allow the red candle to burn itself out.

Stay Out of My Business!

SUPPLIES:
Hyacinth incense
1 brown candle
Yarrow

Cast circle. Light incense. Call up your anger and frustration. Channel it into the candle, transforming it to a barrier. See the barrier as an invisible wall that holds your life and personal business behind it and out of view. Light the candle. Take up the yarrow and drop it into the flame, saying, "Power of yarrow will serve me well, no one sees and none can tell. I now demand my privacy, and as I say it, so it shall be!" Close circle and allow candle to burn out.

Creatively Mad

SUPPLIES:
Medium-size piece of citrine
Cinnamon powder

This spell works best if you use the build-and-transfer technique. Use the stone as a storage facility for your anger for about a week. After that time, place the stone in a dish of cinnamon powder. Put the dish near your work surface and create something. Even if it is only writing in your journal, exercise that muscle in your mind. You will need to cleanse the stone, once the energy feels spent, by burying it in salt or earth for at least a day.

Back Off, Buddy!

SUPPLIES:
1 black candle
Mirror
Black pepper

Cast circle. Build your anger to a frenzied point. Channel it into the candle. Visualize yourself as a fierce warrior. Using the mirror, see yourself confidently telling your attackers, "Back off, Buddy!" Sprinkle black pepper through the flame and say, "And it is so!" and it is.

Dissolve Bad Communication

SUPPLIES:
Nutmeg incense
1 antacid tablet
Small cup of water

Cast circle and light the incense. Take the antacid tablet and carve or write "Bad C" on it. Call up your anger and send it all into the tablet. Hold the tablet until you are sure all the anger is in there. Once it is, drop the tablet into the cup of water and watch it dissolve. Know that the communication lines have now been cleared. This spell really helps in times of a Mercury retrograde.

Destruction of Mental or Emotional Blocks

SUPPLIES:
Patchouli incense
Bell
Chicken bones—dried in the sun for a few days
Mortar and pestle
Small black cloth bag

Cast circle and set incense to smoking. Call up your anger. Focus on the block you wish to destroy. Ring the bell three times. Tell the bones they represent this block and how much you hate them. Place the bones in your mortar and pestle and begin crushing. Say, "I rid myself of you, now and forever! As I crush these bones into dust, so do I crush that which blocks me!" When the bones are dust and your anger is spent, sweep the dust into the black bag. Bury the bag somewhere off of your property.

Bind My Mouth

SUPPLIES:
1 small obsidian stone
1 length black thread

Cast circle. Build your anger and channel into the stone as a zipper. Tie the thread tightly around the stone. See the stone as a representation of "loose lips sinking ships." Say, "With this thread I bind, tightly, that which I should keep to myself, rightly. When I speak, it is in harmony. I will this thread and stone be capable of binding my mouth when words that are not well thought out try to burst forth. As I say it, so it shall be!" Each time you fear you may blurt out something inappropriate, kiss the stone three times and vow, "Words of darkness, words of light, none escape, unless represented right."

Destroy This Pain!

A Break-up Aid

SUPPLIES:
Yew berries
Mortar and pestle

This spell should be done outside, if possible. At night, take your berries and mortar and pestle to a sacred spot and cast circle. Place the berries in the mortar and begin to build your anger at the situation. The berries represent the grieving process you are experiencing, the pestle, and your will to destroy the pain. Begin to smash them and say whatever comes to mind, being very careful to speak to the pain only. When they are smashed beyond all recognition and your anger is spent, exit the circle through your doorway and bury the berries. Return to the circle and spend a few moments contemplating new beginnings and projects. Ask the Great Mother to recycle the energy you buried and use it for the good of all. Close circle.

Hear Me!

SUPPLIES:

1 pen or pencil
1 piece of blank paper
Cauldron or burning dish
Cypress oil
Matches or lighter

Take up the pen and write on the paper, "All will hear me, all will heed, all will notice, I plant the seed. The seed shall grow and all will know, my words are important, I deem it so!" Place the paper in your dish or cauldron and sprinkle it with the cypress oil. Set it on fire. Say, "Glorious fire, carry my desire, it is through you that I release. My will in mind, to be heard until a time, that I ask for it to cease."

Anger + Determination = Success

SUPPLIES:

1 red candle
1 bit of black cloth
Pinch of gold glitter
Bit of patchouli

Cast circle. Build and transfer your anger into the red candle. Visualize it as a tidal wave of determination. See it crash and land as a sprinkling of gold glitter. Drip three drops of the wax onto the center of the cloth. Sprinkle it with glitter. Add a pinch of patchouli and tie the four corners together. Close circle. Carry it with you to remind you of your goals.

27. Rituals

Because this book is not a Magic 101–type book, it assumes you already have a set method for casting a sacred circle. For Anger Magic, however, I recommend calling to the elements directly, as well as beginning your calls with the South. In case you do not have a set system for casting your circle, you can follow this basic circle casting for Anger Magic: Place a red candle in the South. Place a yellow candle in the East. Place a green candle in the North. Place a blue candle in the West. Stand facing the south, lift your arms to the sky, and call out, "I call to the everlasting essence of the South, the true spirit of Fire! I ask that you attend my rite, protect my circle, and hold my magic true!" Light the red candle. Face East, hold your arms skyward and say, "I call to the everlasting essence of the East, the true spirit of Air! I ask that you attend my rite, protect my circle, and hold my magic true!" Light the yellow candle. Face the North, lift your arms skyward, and say, "I call to the everlasting essence of the North, the true spirit of the Earth! I ask that you attend my rite, protect my circle, and hold my magic true!" Light the green candle. Face the West, lift your arms skyward, and say, "I call to the everlasting essence of the West, the true spirit of Water! I ask that you attend my rite, protect my circle, and hold my magic true!" Light the blue candle. When dismissing the elements you should begin in the West. Call out, "Spirit of the West, from which all lifeblood flows, thank you and farewell. I send my blessings with you." Put out the blue candle. Face the North and say, "Spirit of the Earth, from which all life springs, thank you and farewell. I send my blessings with you." Put out the green candle. Face the East and say, "Spirit of the wind, breath of all life, thank you and farewell. I send my blessings with you." Put out the yellow candle. Face the South and say, "Spirit of the South, the warmth of all life, thank you and farewell. I send my blessings with you." Put out the red candle.

In Anger Magic, a circle is necessary for every spell, ritual, exercise, and meditation that you perform. Pay particular attention in your circle calls to the placement of barriers.

Specific barriers can help control the flow of magic. When you are calling each element, ask for your barrier to be upheld. For example, if you were to say, "I call upon the element of Fire to attend my rite and send your aid," the timing would be appropriate to add, "By the purity of your nature I ask you to hold my magic pure. May it not stray into ———— [the area of danger as determined from the magical laws in chapter 1]."

Anger Magic rituals are somewhat informal, yet you should take every possible precaution to ensure the intent does not stray. Other essential elements when working with Anger Magic include cleansing yourself and the area before and after magical work, grounding before and after, and following all necessary safety precautions.

A special note about blood work in angry rituals: I do not recommend bloodletting while employing anger in magic. Granted, blood is a valuable item and has its place in magic, but combining blood with anger often has a violent effect. If you insist on trying it, at least have someone else watch over you for a few days. Bloodletting is never necessary, it is optional. We can accomplish the same purpose by using a substitute for blood. However, I realize that many people feel a deeper connection with their magic when they employ blood. If you feel you must use blood, then I suggest you wait until the anger has been successfully transformed back into raw energy.

The Darker Side of Life Tarot Ritual

In chapter 1, we discussed a ritual that would allow you to place yourself in the shoes of another. That is the function of this Darker Side of Life Tarot Ritual. To perform it correctly, it is imperative to clearly understand its purpose and its backlash. We will attempt communication to the person's higher self to get into his subconscious. The full circle effect that such an action will have is severe. You get no cushion and have to go into this knowing that. Attempting to excuse yourself from the full-circle effect will assure that the ritual will fail. It has to be done with a willingness to open yourself to whatever adversity the divine wishes to bestow on you. This willingness proves your goodwill to the other person's higher self.

Even though you get no cushion, you should take every precaution you possibly can, to avoid involving others. This ritual is not to be taken lightly. While carrying it out is relatively simple, it is nonetheless a very powerful and manipulative magical task. Be aware of the risks. Have a good cleansing ritual to perform immediately following this. Make sure to ground yourself well.

To perform this ritual you will need a cleansed and consecrated space.

SUPPLIES:

Divination oil; in this case I highly recommend
    carnation oil
Oil warmer, one that uses a tea light candle
Black candle
White candle
Yellow candle
2 separate glasses of juice or water
Mirror
Tarot deck
Bloodstone
Hematite
Anointing oil

The altar setup is simple. The black candle will be on the upper left corner. Place the white candle in the upper right corner. In between the two candles place the oil warmer. Directly in front of the warmer, place the yellow candle. Underneath the yellow candle, place the tarot cards. To the right of the cards place your stones and to the left, the mirror. Place the glasses together a little above the tarot cards.

Black Candle

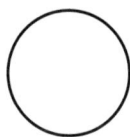

Oil Warmer

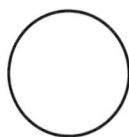

White Candle

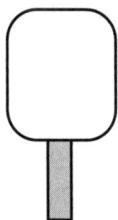

Mirror

Yellow Candle

Stones

Goblets

Tarot Cards

The Altar Setup

To begin, cast your circle. Settle yourself comfortably within it. Place the divination oil in the warmer and light the tea light candle to warm the oil. Anoint the black candle and charge it with absorbing. Its duty is to soak up any negative energy surrounding your work. Anoint the white candle and charge it with goodwill. Its duty is to surround the working with harmonious circumstances. Anoint the yellow candle and charge it with the power of communication. Its duty is to establish a link between your higher self and the higher self of the person you are performing the working for.

Hold one glass of the juice or water up in offering to your higher self. When speaking with the higher self (both yours and theirs) always do so while looking in a mirror for this ritual. Say something along the lines of, "I speak now to my higher self, who knows my life purpose and goals. I come to you hoping to facilitate contact with one I love, hoping to honor you in my actions. I send you to his higher self to bring this to me." Place the glass back on the table.

Raise the second glass of the juice or water to offer it to the other higher self. Say something along the lines of, "You know my heart, for I lay it bare before you. I am willing to take on any consequences for this action; I believe in it that much. The one you guide is the one I love and I wish for entry so that I may see and I may know his hurts and heal them. I open to give you willingly anything within me you may desire to take. Show me." Say everything it is in your heart to say to his higher self. Then set the glass down and take up the tarot cards. You will be doing a spread designed specifically to show you the person's dark side.

All cards will lay out on the left, so begin with the first card in close proximity to you placed to the far right. The second will lie above it. The third will lie to the left and start the second column, at the bottom. In the second column, you will lay cards 3, 4, and 5, one on top of the other with the fifth card being on top. Shift left again and lay cards 6, 7, and 8, with 6 on the bottom and 8 at the top.

```
┌──────┐   ┌──────┐
│      │   │      │
│  8   │   │  5   │        ┌──────┐
│      │   │      │        │      │
└──────┘   └──────┘        │  2   │
                           │      │
┌──────┐   ┌──────┐        └──────┘
│      │   │      │
│  7   │   │  4   │        ┌──────┐
│      │   │      │        │      │
└──────┘   └──────┘        │  1   │
                           │      │
┌──────┐   ┌──────┐        └──────┘
│      │   │      │
│  6   │   │  3   │
│      │   │      │
└──────┘   └──────┘
```

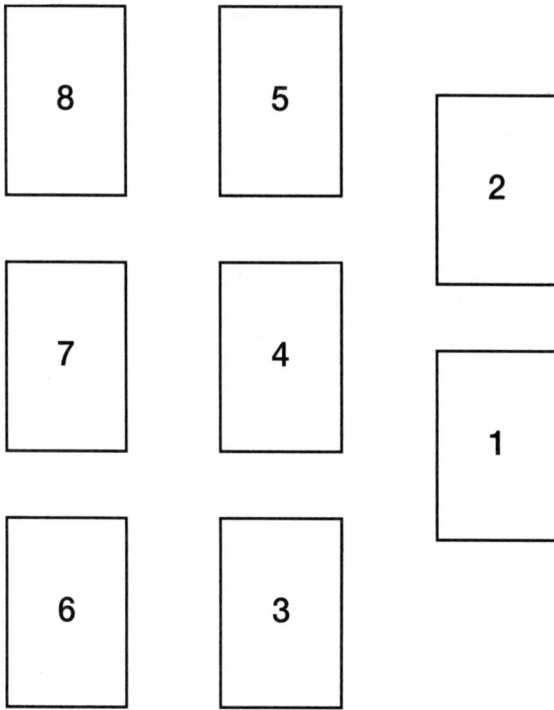

Dark Side Tarot Layout

- Card 1 represents the state of the other person at this moment.
- Card 2 represents the deepest and darkest emotion he is dealing with currently.
- Card 3 represents the past events that are influencing the situation.
- Card 4 represents his biggest block in life.
- Card 5 represents the darkest trait within him.
- Card 6 represents the biggest strength within him.
- Card 7 represents the area of the downfall.
- Card 8 represents what may consume him. Any unhealthy obsessions would end up here.

You may be surprised at the insights this spread can show you. By obtaining the help of the higher self (both yours and his) you should find yourself standing squarely in the other person's shoes. Stay long enough to do what it is you came to do. When you are done, gather the cards together and stack them back into the deck. Say aloud to the other person's higher self, "Thank you and blessings! I will never reveal that which I have learned to anyone. I leave now." That is a promise you will want to make sure you keep forever. Say to your higher self, "Thank you and blessings! I leave now."

Before you close circle you may want to record your sensations in your Book of Shadows. Spend some time reflecting in the mirror to gain additional insight into yourself. After you feel you have recorded all you want you may put out the candles and put your things away. Keep the memories as treasures of your friend. Close circle.

Conjuring a Fire Circle

The purpose of this ritual is to aid you if you are having trouble reaching a decision on a justice matter. Kali-Ma, a formidable force, will aid you, but there may be a price to pay. So we will assume that there is a price and offer a token in advance. Kali loves to be catered to. She is the wild force behind everything after all, so the token must be something we truly wish to keep. And yes, we will give it to her.

Find a suitable object and be sure that the decision requires her help and that you are not giving away a personal treasure for something you don't care that much about.

You will need a cleansed and consecrated space, preferably outside. Line the perimeter in a circle with novena-type candles. Place jasmine incense at each of the cardinal directions. You will need a glass of cool water and a pan of warm water. Other helpful items are perfumes and fresh flowers. Carry the water into the circle. Light the incense and candles and cast your circle.

When your circle is cast, sit comfortably within it. Rest for a moment and then stand. Starting at the south walk the perimeter of the circle Deosil. Do this continually while thinking about the situation you need help with. Allow yourself to be angry. Feel the ground getting warmer with each step you take. Visualize flames erupting behind you until the circle is a ring of fire.

When you feel the moment is right, say something along the lines of, "Kali-Ma, my dark mother. I know that you are here with me. I bring you cool water to drink and warm water so that I may wash your feet." Now offer the drinking water to Kali, and then you take a sip. Dip a cloth into the warm water. Wring it out onto the ground, and then wash your feet. Say, "I am with you now. I honor you. I know you will speak to my heart. What should I do about ———?" Slowly spray the perfume on the ground and on yourself. Offer your trinket to Kali by burying it. Tell her it is hers.

Be patient and pay attention, it is not likely that you will miss her, but since we are calling her within a context (as a part of us) she may speak quite gently. When you have heard what you needed to hear thank her and close circle. Leave the trinket where it sits. You may never reclaim it; it is hers now.

Calling Anger Home

The purpose of this ritual is to call home any anger that you may have allowed to slip through the cracks. Often you can be so harried that this can happen without your realization. It is a good habit to perform this ritual every so often to maintain the perfect control you strive for. You do not want your power out there in the hands of others to use, as they will when you are not certain their goals match yours.

SUPPLIES:
Frankincense incense
1 white candle
1 red candle

Call Your Anger Home Oil (page 205)
Magnet
Black sand (if you can't get black sand you can use either
   black cotton fabric or regular sand)

The altar is set up with the candles placed in the center. Set them side by side, with the red on the left and the white on the right. They should be touching. The sand is placed directly in front of the candles, with the magnet in the center of the sand. The incense can be placed on the left, just wherever you like.

Light the incense. Cast circle. Anoint the candles with the oil. Touch the magnet with a drop of the oil. The white candle represents you. The red candle represents your anger. Say, "What I have unintentionally released, I now call home. Any and all angry energy that is mine, I ask to be returned to me to deal with. I accept responsibility for my emotions."

Light the white candle. Say, "By the lighting of this flame, this candle symbolizes me. I seek no cover and do not wish to hide from my actions." Light the red candle. Say, "By the lighting of this flame, this candle calls my anger home to me. It is mine to deal with and no other's." Pick up the red candle and drip the wax, one drop at a time, onto the white candle. With each drop say, "Flames unite, to do what is right. Return to me, my responsibility." Continue dripping the wax until the white candle is covered with red spots. Turn the red candle upside down into the sand to extinguish the flame and set it to the side.

Move the white candle forward and arrange the sand around it. Drip wax from the white candle onto the magnet. Place the magnet directly in front of the candle. Allow the candle to burn itself out while you write in your journal or on paper any possible instances where your anger may have seeped out and what you plan to do with it now. Once the candle goes out, close circle and clean up.

This ritual may be incorporated as a prelude to another purpose—such as, if you need to perform a spell for some reason, you would do so immediately after the writing portion of the ritual.

Destruction

The ritual of destruction is exactly that. Its purpose is to disintegrate any negative influences or circumstances. This ritual makes use of anger-building techniques and explosives. It should only be performed outdoors. Extreme caution is advised. I recommend driving iron stakes in the perimeter of your circle.

SUPPLIES:
Fire circle; with a fire already burning
1 black candle
Eat My Problem oil (page 200)
Hollowed-out eggshell
End This NOW! powder (page 200)
What you wish to destroy written on paper
Firecracker

Cast circle. Sit on the ground before the fire and spread your items around you. Anoint the candle with the Eat My Problem oil. Light it and place it in a holder on the ground. Take the eggshell and say, "This represents the problem, after tonight it shall exist no longer!" Seal one end of the eggshell with the wax from the candle and load the End This NOW! powder and the paper with the problem written on it into the shell. Stuff the firecracker into the shell with the fuse sticking out of the end. Seal around the fuse with candle wax, but leave a tiny bit of room for oxygen to get in.

Use your favorite anger-building technique if needed to build your anger to a high level. Once you feel the rush of anger come over you, channel it all into the eggshell. It is normal to wish to yell as the energy leaves your body and goes into the shell.

Touch the fuse sticking out of the eggshell to the candle to light it and quickly toss it into the fire. You should hear a small explosion from the firecracker. This represents the destruction of the problem, it is now gone. Allow the fire to burn out and clean up. You should follow this with a thorough cleansing and make sure to ground properly.

Transformation

Keep in mind that anger changes when it reaches our minds. It goes into attack mode. If we do not give it an object to attack, frequently it will attack what it can reach—us.

Transformation rituals can be—and should be—lengthy processes. They are simple, but require time and effort. Introspection is key during any transformation ritual. The process of transforming clouded emotion back to pure energy requires that we remove the coloring we placed on it. Therefore, we must know the anger inside and out and determine its true stem.

Meditation during transformation rituals is important. The pattern we will follow to accomplish the transformation is:

Cast circle
Call anger out
Examine anger thoroughly (meditation)
Release coloring
Examine again
Put into action

For example, a few years back a neighbor was cleaning his gun. The gun accidentally went off and shot through my walls, lodging in my hot water heater. I was awakened by the sound of people banging on my door to see whether I was okay. I answered the door half asleep and was told that my house had been shot. Then I noticed all the water on the floor.

I looked a bit closer and a rage came over me when I realized that had it not been for the water heater, my daughter or myself could easily have been shot in our sleep, in our own home. The water heater had stopped the bullet; the bed we were sleeping in was directly in its path.

I was so enraged that the police told the neighbor to go stay somewhere else for his own safety. In my fury, I had told them flat out that had that bullet touched my child, the man would not have taken another breath. I meant it too.

After the shock wore off and I went to work dealing with the anger, I employed the method presented here. I cast my circle and called my anger out by speaking directly to it. I studied it hard and what I found at the root was not pretty.

I was angry because the foolish man had almost harmed my child. I was angry about it because it would have hurt me. I was threatened by the mere thought of losing one I loved so dearly. In addition, I was severely pissed that no one else seemed to grasp the horror of what *could* have happened. Everyone else focused on the fact that we were not hurt and completely skimmed over the part where our home had been shot because of the stupidity of another's actions. I felt invalidated because no one understood the emotions involved for me.

Upon seeing all of this at the root, I then had to release the coloring of the emotion. I had colored my anger as wrong by choosing to see a selfish response pattern—in other words, focusing on myself. Because no one else understood I thought it must be bad to see it in such a way. I had been allowing others to label my emotions as inactive by accepting their viewpoint. The fact of the matter is that anger is individual; it is unavoidable to see a selfish pattern. However, it is not selfish in the least, it is supposed to be perceived that way. Emotions relate to the individual; they are valid through their very existence. The only point of view that matters is the one of the person experiencing it.

In order to achieve transformation, I had to release the coloring. Out loud, I proclaimed that I had every right to be mad about this and to take action. I examined it again with new eyes that allowed for the purity of the energy to shine through. When I did, I chose to put it into action as a protective shield for my daughter, since that was the area in which I felt threatened. I did this by stating aloud, "Through divinity I have been instilled with an immense power. I have been gifted with energy aplenty to protect my family. I choose to do so now!" and I visualized a wall about three feet thick surrounding my daughter. That was three years ago and the wall is still there. Every time I think about the incident today, the image of the wall just gets bigger from the emotion I still feed it. The whole process took several days. I simply carted my circle with me throughout my workdays and carried on. No one knew what I was doing in my mind.

You can use any sort of informal ritual such as the above example to accomplish the goal of transformation. If you wish to transform anger sent to you via someone else, the process can be the same, with the exception of whose emotion you are viewing. Transforming anger sent from others can be time consuming. You may have to carry it awhile.

There is an easier way: You may accomplish the transformation by using an absorbent poppet. Sew the poppet and stuff it with charcoal.

Add a "link," which can be bits of hair or nail clippings, or a slip of paper with the person's name written on it. Throw in a quartz crystal for the heart. Seal the poppet, and charge it with the ability to absorb the emotion sent your way. Allow it to do so undisturbed for twenty-four hours. Build a fire outside and cast circle. Call to activate the anger inside the doll. Say, "Power was sent to me and meant to cause harm. I do not allow this! I employ this emotion to do the function of ————. Through my will, as it has been gifted to me, it will follow my instruction now and forever more. So mote it be!" You may burn the doll or bury it. If you bury it, the doll will rot in time, the heart of it (quartz) will not. Simple methods such as this work best for transforming the anger of others. Transforming our own is a bit more complicated.

Transformation takes place on a personal level. A "pull out all the stops" ritual is not required; it is optional. What is not optional is the amount of time it takes. If it takes a week, then it takes a week. Do not rush it. For that reason it is best to keep your transformation rituals informal, so that you may work with them and simultaneously carry on your daily life.

The lightning bolt is a common symbol for anger. As it also signifies change a simple transformation ritual can be to trace a lightning bolt into sand or salt with your finger or athame, erase it, and draw the corresponding symbol for the goal you wish to focus the energy on. For example, if you wish to direct your energy to love you could morph the lightning bolt into a heart.

The Three C's: A Transformation Ritual

SUPPLIES:
1 gray candle
Cypress oil
Calamus—about a teaspoon or less
Cinquefoil—about three small pinches

Cast your circle. Make sure to place any barriers that are needed. Meditate on why you are angry and what you would like to do with the energy. Once you feel sufficiently angry, channel the emotion into the candle. Anoint the candle with the cypress oil. Call out, "It is my will to transform my anger into raw power, so that I may put it to use improving my life." Light the candle. Lift your arms skyward and call out, "Mother Hecate! As you transform all things and hold the keys to enlightenment, I ask that you wrap your loving arms around me and aid me in my rite. I watch now as this energy undergoes the eternal cycle of death and rebirth under your watchful eye. As your child, I ask that you hold this energy true to the purpose I wish to use it for. Allow none of it to stray elsewhere." Take a pinch of the calamus and drop it into the flame. As you drop it chant, "Bit by bit, drop by drop, feelings of hostility, come to a stop." Continue in this fashion until you have used all of the calamus. Take a pinch of cinquefoil and drop it into the flame. As you do, say, "I control the energy, it is mine to use as I will." Drop another pinch of cinquefoil into the flame and say, "I direct this energy to ———. It will work to bring peace and harmony into my life." Drop the last pinch of cinquefoil into the flame and say, "I choose for this energy to be put to use as a ———. It will heal and harmonize my spirit. As I speak it, so shall it be!"

28. Grimoire

In the grimoire, you will find specific recipes and suggested herbal combinations. The reason for this is some people will wish to perform fire magic, others will prefer to use potions, and still others may prefer powders. The combination lists can be worked into whichever form best suits you.

For potions, you may use either an oil, water, or an alcohol base. The same goes for elixirs, of course. For powders, I prefer a charcoal base, but you may use rice powder (rice powder multiplies the power of the herbs). I suggest using a castor-and-vegetable-oil combination for your base oil, as castor has absorbing qualities and will hold the magic within itself. For alcohol, you can use regular over-the-counter isopropyl (rubbing) alcohol or vodka.

I strongly recommend a thirty-day resting period for your brews, but it is not essential. If you find yourself in need, you may use these mixtures right away. Adding a touch of benzoin or a benzoin tincture acts as a preservative to keep your brews from spoiling.

At no time should you attempt to ingest or place on your skin any of the recipes that contain herbs marked as poisonous in chapter 25.

Hexing Powder

> Pinch of graveyard dirt
> Iron filings (preferably rusty)
> Powdered sulfur
> Black pepper

Combine all ingredients. You may add a pinch of gunpowder, if you wish. If you do, make sure to add it last, after all of the other ingredients are already powdered together. Write the problem down on paper and sprinkle this powder on it. Wind the paper tightly around the powder. Burn or bury.

End This NOW!

Graveyard dirt
Iron filings
Black pepper
Basil
Sulfur
Loosestrife
Gunpowder

End This NOW! is used to put a complete, albeit abrupt, end to something. The optimal condition for making this powder is on a stormy, dark moon night. Combine graveyard dirt, iron filings, black pepper, basil, sulfur and loosestrife together in your mortar. Using the pestle in a widdershins pattern, powder the herbs. Add a pinch of gunpowder last. Burn it to be rid of the problem.

Eat My Problem Oil

Nettles
Venus flytrap
Oil

Crush a handful of nettles and one bud of a Venus flytrap. Soak in oil for thirty days in a cool, dark place. Strain for use.

To Freeze Something

Powdered camphor
Alcohol
Jasmine
Paper for writing on

Soak powdered camphor in alcohol. Add a pinch of jasmine if desired. Keep capped tightly and allow to rest for thirty days. On a slip of paper, write what you wish to freeze, and soak the paper in the liquid. Place it in the freezer. When you are ready, you may burn it, giving you the power of both fire and ice working in your favor.

War Water

War water is used to create a hostile environment. It works well for building purposes and can also be used as a hexing agent.

Water
Rusty nails
Tobacco
Pinch of patchouli leaves
Pinch of powdered sulfur
Glass jar

Combine all the ingredients in the glass jar. Allow the ingredients time to meld, usually about thirty days. Store the mixture in a dark cool place. When you are ready to use it you must break the glass jar by throwing it at the object you wish to destroy (if hexing). If using for building purposes War Water may be simmered in a potpourri pot.

Four Thieves Vinegar

Four Thieves Vinegar is used as a hexing agent. Simply write the problem on paper and soak the paper in the liquid. Allow it to dry and burn. Load the ashes into a black candle if you wish and banish it.

1 bottle apple cider vinegar
Rosemary
Wormwood
Rue

Camphor
Patchouli

Add to the bottle of apple cider vinegar the list of ingredients (in handfuls). Heat the mixture to the point of boiling for four days in a row. Strain and keep tightly capped. Store in a cool dark place.

Hexing Oil

Black pepper
Wormwood
Oil

Mix equal amounts of black pepper and wormwood together. Cover with oil. Allow to sit for thirty days in a cool dark place. Strain.

Controlling Oil

Calumus
Oil

Soak calamus in oil for thirty days. Strain. Use it when you need to gain better self-control by applying one drop on the top of your head.

Cool Anger Potion

Passionflower
Rose petals
Orris root
Sugar
Honey
Alcohol

Mix together the first five ingredients. Cover with alcohol and let sit for thirty days. Strain.

To Sour a Situation

Vinegar
Lemon juice
Glass bottle
Paper to write on

Mix together equal parts vinegar and lemon juice in a glass bottle. Write the situation you wish to sour on paper. Place the paper inside the bottle, and cap it tightly.

To Honor Hecate

Sandalwood
Cypress
Patchouli
Alcohol

Combine the first three ingredients and place in alcohol. Let rest for thirty days. Burn in your cauldron to honor Hecate.

To Stimulate Aggression

Black pepper
Benzoin
Pine needles

Combine the ingredients in equal portions and burn.

For Aid in Building Anger

Clove
Black pepper
Dragon's blood

Combine the ingredients in equal portions and burn.

To Honor Pele

Frankincense
Dragon's blood
Sandalwood
Orange
Clove
Cinnamon

Throw by handfuls into a fire.

To Instill Courage

Ginger
Clove
Black pepper
Oil
1 red candle

Soak the ingredients in oil for thirty days. Strain and anoint a red candle to call for courage.

To Break a Habit

Rosemary
Sage
Lemon juice

Powder the herbs and squeeze the lemon juice over the powder. Let the herbs absorb the juice. Once dry, you may sprinkle this where it would best suit—such as on cigarettes if you are trying to quit smoking, for example.

To Repair a Spell Gone Wrong

Bay leaves
Frankincense
Oil
1 white candle

Crush the herbs and soak in oil for thirty days. Anoint a white candle and call upon divinity to repair the spell.

Call Your Anger Home

Bay
Rosemary
Cayenne pepper
Oil
Magnet

Powder the ingredients and soak in oil. Let rest in a dark, cool place for thirty days. This oil works faster if you allow a magnet to rest the original thirty days with it.

Curse-Breaking Herbal Combinations

Throw the combination lists together in equal parts and burn to be rid of negative vibrations.

FORMULA 1:
Sandalwood
Bay

FORMULA 2:
Sandalwood
Bay
Rosemary
Yarrow

FORMULA 3:
Frankincense
Rosemary
Dragon's blood

Magical Fires

FOR DESTRUCTION:
Willow
Yew wood

FOR TRANSFORMATION:
Holly
Hazel
Hornbeam

FOR PROTECTION:
Redwood
Cedar

FOR HEALING:
Ash
Beech
Maple

FOR POWER:
Ebony
Oak
Poplar

FOR DIVINATION:
Sandalwood
Juniper
Cedar

Clichés That Work

Piss and vinegar: Yes, it is a pretty disgusting combo. However, we can find its roots in folk magic, most notably Hoodoo. Simply bottle the urine and add vinegar. You should use a glass bottle; an old soda bottle works fine. This solution will sour any situation. You may make use of it by either writing the problem on paper and inserting it into the bottle, or throwing the bottle at the object you wish to sour (or a representation of it).

Piss me off: Continuing in this disagreeable vein there is this cliché, which is also based in folk magic. Urine has the ability to banish problems. Sealing urine in a bottle with a representation of the problem has a binding effect.

Bad blood: A drop of lemon juice mixed with a drop of blood will sour the person's disposition.

Spill the beans: Spilling beans can be used in divination to learn the truth about a situation. Simply toss and scry for possible shapes.

BIBLIOGRAPHY

Bullfinch, Thomas. *Bulfinch's Mythology; The Illustrated Age of Fable*. Stewart, Tabori & Chang, 1998.

Cabot, Laurie. *Power of the Witch*. Bantam Doubleday Dell Publishing Group, 1989.

Cunningham, Scott. *The Complete Book of Incense, Oils and Brews*. Llewellyn Publications, 1989.

Cunningham, Scott. *Cunningham's Encyclopedia of Crystal, Gem and Metal Magic*. Llewellyn Worldwide, 1987.

————. *Cunningham's Encyclopedia of Magical Herbs*. Llewellyn Worldwide, 1984.

————. *Hawaiian Magic and Spirituality*. Llewellyn Publications, 2001.

Davidson, H.R. Ellis. *Scandinavian Mythology*. The Hamlyn Publishing Group, 1982.

Euripides. *Medea*.

Graves, Robert. *Greek Gods And Heroes*. Dell-Laurel Leaf, 1960.

————. *Greek Myths*. Penguin, 1955.

Hamilton, Edith. *The Greek Way*. W.W. Norton and Company, 1943.

Hendricks, Rhoda A. *Classical Gods and Heroes*. Morrow Quill Paperbacks, 1972.

Holland, Eileen. *The Wicca Handbook*. Samuel Weiser, 2000.

Homer. *The Odyssey*.

Jordan, Michael. *The Encyclopedia of GODS*. Facts on File, 1993.

Marlborough, Ray T. *Charms, Spells and Formulas*. Llewellyn Publications, 1986.

Moura, Anne. *Green Witchcraft II; Balancing Light and Shadow*. Llewellyn Publications, 1999.

New Larousse Encyclopedia of Mythology. The Hamlyn Publishing Group, 1970.

Pinsent, John. *Greek Mythology*. The Hamlyn Publishing Group, 1969.

Stassinopoulos, Arianna, and Roloff Beny. *The Gods of Greece*. Wiedenfeld & Nicholson, 1983.

Wilkinson, Philip. *The Illustrated Dictionary of Mythology*. DK Publishing, 1998.

Wolf, Christa. *Medea*. Doubleday (Bantam), 1998.

INDEX